SOULMERGING™

THE PATH OF HEALING

THE FIRST TABLET OF TESTIMONY

SOULMERGING™

THE PATH OF HEALING

THE FIRST TABLET OF TESTIMONY

Humanity has begun to discover the living light of the soul.

Dr. Frank Stainetti

Phone: 805-897-0011
Email: Soulmerginginfo@gmail.com
Website: www.soulmerging.com
Address: P.O. Box 5222
Santa Barbara, CA 93150

Published by Moment of Light Publishing, a division of The Momentum of Light, Inc., P.O. Box 5222, Santa Barbara, California 93150

The Momentum of Light is a non-profit foundation.

ISBN-13: 978-1466412712

CONTENTS

Author's Note

The story I am about to share with you is as profound as it is deep, unbelievable and yet real. It is the story of my life, and the journey I took to heal the emotional wounds of my past, discover the light of my soul and the attainment of an enlightened state of Christ Consciousness. While this is my story, in truth, the teachings and revelations are meant for everyone. Walk with me through the pages of my life and discover how to face and heal your emotional wounds and enter the Soulmerging experience. This experience is permanently life changing. One is imbued with a new capacity for love, dramatic new levels of peace and a new found ability to see the beauty in yourself, others and the world.

As I look back over my life, I realize that I have always carried a passionate feeling within me, a feeling of intense love for the beauty in all things, yet everyone around me was filled with stress, sorrow, depression, illness, anger and personal dramas. People appeared to be blindly going through the motions of their mundane lives, never feeling fulfilled and at peace—just surviving from one day to the next. It didn't take long for the circumstance of my abusive home-life to directly affect me. After years of strife and abuse, I felt a profound and deep longing to find myself. My "being" was fragmented, as if I were some place very far away. Loving the beauty around me was easy, but I didn't know how to let love in. I wanted to find my way to that far away place, but how would I get there? My despair felt like a hole that could not be filled; yet, at the same time, my passion to be in love with everything was like breathing. I felt deep despair and a longing to "find myself." I looked for answers but I couldn't find them in the outside world. It seemed nothing I did brought insight, answers or solutions to the state my life was in. Outwardly, I had achieved the American dream, complete with a home at the beach, a successful business and a family. This perfect exterior was all a facade. One day at the peak of my success, a deep emptiness came over me, a sort of mental breakdown. At this same moment, it was as if the presence of God, a much greater presence then me, began to direct my life. It was at this time Archangel Gabriel came into my life as a teacher and a guild.

In the early eighties, I took some time off from work and went to visit some friends. In their guest room was a book about spiritual transformation; intrigued, I picked it up and began reading. The main character was discovering that the answers to her most difficult life questions were revealed by going within. "Going within," I thought. And so it was, at this moment, my journey began and my life was forever changed.

I was inspired, and at the same time, I was afraid to look inside myself for fear of what I might find. There were so many painful memories. I thought, "Why should I go there?" I felt my resistance; however, I wondered if the memories were somehow the doorway leading to understanding, healing and a new life. It was more than self-discovery; I longed to know why I felt so far away from myself. The Divine presence of Gabriel was compelling me to go deep within myself and remember who I am. I had no idea where it was going to lead, but I had nowhere else to turn.

Once I began, my journey became a profound awakening. It unveiled not only the deep emotional wounds from my childhood of abuse and neglect, it accelerated into a continuous expanded spiritual awareness and lightness of being. The burdens I had been carrying were lifting and permanently transmuting. I was awakening to who I truly AM and found myself on the path toward enlightenment.

I spent time in solitude. I meditated several times a day and I attended healing events around the country. After studying with healers and shamans and after attending healing events, I started to notice a light within me. It was like a Divine spark within me. I could literally see this flicker of light in my mind's eye and I could feel the love within it. It came spontaneously, sometimes during my healing experiences and meditation, and it was an amazing thing because it felt like intense love, and love had been absent from my life. As I experienced this wonderful "love and light," I began to have soul memories of living before, but it was more than that, it was as if I was gathering soul wisdom that had been dormant within me. I continued to be guided and directed by Archangel Gabriel and I began to find the answers I was seeking. It was so fulfilling. I kept going deeper and deeper within myself and uncovered a mountain of pain. The more I understood the source or event causing the pain, the more accelerated my healing became. The more I healed, the more I experienced the love and Divine light within me. As time went on I realized that I was merging with the light of my soul. It was alive, illuminating and filled with love. Prior to this time, I had only heard we have a "soul," not ever really understanding what it was or if it really existed. But now I had the direct experience of my own soul. Then it happened, I fully entered the Soulmerging experience, a heart opening so extraordinary it changed my life forever. Jesus (Yeshua) appeared stating this was just the beginning and began to reveal the secrets of his life and how to further access "Heaven on Earth."

This story is much more than my story of healing. This book is a revelation about the path to healing and the enlightenment achieved by Jesus (Yeshua) that is available to all of us. Through my journey, the truths about Jesus, the Cross, the Holy Grail and our Divine purpose were revealed. While I realize the information will be strongly rejected by the Christian community, I am compelled to share it with you, for you are free to choose what to believe or not believe.

Jesus was not "The Son of God" as all Christian faiths proclaim. We are all children of God. He was elevated as the Divine son of God, making his state of enlightenment unattainable by others. This is untrue! Jesus was a man who achieved enlightenment—the union of the Divine love and light within, which is a living state of beingness known as Christ Consciousness. Jesus never intended to be elevated beyond any other human being. Rather, he demonstrated the example of what is possible for each and every one of us. He told his disciples they would do everything he could do and more. He called them "The light of the World." Through my path of healing, I discovered the path Jesus took into Christ Consciousness. Although this flies in the face of Christianity, the life and path of fear, judgment and suffering is not necessary. Jesus' life example and teachings are the "Living Way" for us all. However, the truth of his message was distorted, modified and hidden from all humanity.

We've all heard about the "Quest for the Holy Grail." During my journey into Christ Consciousness, I discovered the truth about the missing cup. The Holy Grail is not a physical cup at all; the Holy Grail is within you. You, I and every other human being are the Holy Grail—if we so choose. "The Kingdom of Heaven is within." We have the potential, or the choice, to become the cup that overfloweth. This is part of the secret that was kept from us, leaving us with the false premise that we are not Divine and that our humanity is a mental prison, a life of sin sentencing us to a life of repentance. In the Ten Commandments it states, "Thou shalt have no other gods before me." This includes gurus and priests; there is no intermediary between you and God.

The path Jesus took was not easy. Even He entered the path of healing, transmuting emotional pain, fear and terror. Jesus was a man with a mate, Mary Magdalene, he was an Essene and He was "Light Incepted," as were all the Essenes. Immaculate Conception or "Light Inception" was not unique to Jesus. During the lost years of Jesus, Archangel Gabriel directed and guided Him to many ancient sites on his path of healing. He was human as we are human. He, however, faced the depth of his emotional wounding to demonstrate the path to achieving Christ Consciousness. And so He did!

We keep Jesus on the Cross and view Him as the representation of suffering and punishment for sins. This is not what the Cross represents at all. Take Jesus off the Cross for the true meaning of the Cross is to unify our four bodies of human existence and enter the purity of love. The four bodies of existence are physical, emotional, mental, and spiritual. To remain on the Cross is to remain in self judgment, condemnation and darkness. By taking Jesus off the Cross we remove the hold of suffering placed upon us by religious dogma. We shatter the illusion of false religious teachings that divide and conquer. Take the Christ off the Cross and remove the belief we are here to suffer.

I hope I can fill in the missing information, or the information that was withheld from us by religious organizations and dogma. Jesus' teachings were meant to assist every man, woman and child in achieving the awakening of the soul light living within. We all have the ability to do this, as He did, by going within, remembering the light of our soul, turning from the false truth of suffering, and walking into the love that was always available to us for all eternity.

Walk with me through the pain of my early years and into the moment of the discovery of my soul light and the threshold of enlightenment. Your part in the enlightenment of all humanity and the second coming is presented to you in this book. I hope you will embrace the truth and walk the path that Jesus had intended for you.

I am not an angel, a sage or a mystic; I am simply a man who has had Divine encounters too numerous to count. My story is the recounting of my personal journey toward healing and achieving Christed Consciousness, my relationship with what we as man term the Divine, and the messages and truths coming from them, through me. I hope you will embrace all that is presented. It will be at times overwhelming as it was for me. But my hope is that as you read this material, the truth of the information will resonate within you and spur you on to your awakening.

Dr. Frank Stainetti

November 2011

SOULMERGING™

THE PATH OF HEALING

THE FIRST TABLET OF TESTIMONY

Split the wood and you will find me. Lift the stone and I will be there . . . The Kingdom of Heaven is within.

— The lost gospel

CHAPTER 1

MY GREATEST TEACHER

There are earth angels all around us. They work in the most unsuspecting ways; they could be a friend, a relative, a stranger, even a child. The presence of the divine is everywhere. The only question is do we have the presence of heart to recognize and receive this blessing?

In the days just before my son Michael was born, I sat in the all-glass office of my penthouse suite, reviewing my life's accomplishments. I had really made it! I was living the American Dream—a beach house with miraculous views, a maid to tend it, Porsche sports cars, plenty of guy-toys, a beautiful young wife, a baby on the way, and plans for more children. I was a successful banker who had accumulated a lot by age 30. The memories of growing up on welfare and missing out on any form of a happy childhood had fueled my ambition and an unrelenting drive to succeed. I promised myself, while growing up, I would realize the American dream and possess every comfort money could buy. More importantly, I believed this material foundation would enable me to create the perfect loving family I so longed for and fantasized about since childhood. As I pondered the early years of my life, I realized that in order to survive the abuse I simply lived in the future all the time; never living in the moment of any day due to the presence of fear that prevailed in our home. To survive this fear and abuse as a child, I created and lived for the future and the dream that I would somehow be happy once I achieved success. That moment was now! However, the illusion I created and lived in was about to shatter.

Suddenly during that last thought about my youth, I felt a strange and deep emptiness well up inside of me. Was I having some sort of breakdown? I wasn't sure. My drive and ambition, without reason, were suddenly gone, erased, as if some greater power had come along and veiled what I thought was the best part of me. Days went by; I thought I should be fine by now, but this strange absence of who I had been, grew stronger. I didn't know myself without my will to succeed. I felt like my personality had vanished, leaving me in a state of complete emptiness. I didn't tell anyone, not even my wife, for fear of looking weak. I withdrew even further, because I did not understand what I was experiencing, and yet I had to appear strong as I was running a company and I had a wife who was about to give birth to our first child. Weeks went by, and I couldn't shake the empty feeling. How was it possible for me to have so much material wealth yet feel so vacant? The emptiness remained right up to the day I received the news that my beautiful newborn son, Michael, would have a severe genetic defect which would cut his life short. This news further shattered the futuristic dream life I had created since childhood.

With the birth of Michael, I met one of my greatest teachers. Even before he arrived, his spiritual presence was entering my awareness. My old lifestyle was falling away, but I didn't know why. I was about to embark upon an astonishing spiritual journey that would not only change my life forever but also reveal the secret that has eluded most religious quests for 2000 years—a leap in consciousness that connects oneself directly to the soul!

Thanks to Michael, for the first time in my life I was truly immersed in all-consuming feelings of love. His arrival awarded a reprieve from the strange emptiness that had begun to plague me. It was such a joy to feed, change and hold him. In the second and third months of his life, something amazing started to happen. When we were alone, angelic bursts of white light would appear in the room. My body would feel electrified with intense energy and my hair would stand on end! It was hard to accept at first, but it happened so often that I got used to it. A radiance of light and the presence of magnificent love flowed from my son continuously and appeared to be growing in magnitude. I realized my heart was opening. At the same time I was shaken to realize just how shut down my heart had become. Tears would stream from my eyes every time I looked at him! Oddly, this would only happen when Michael and I were alone together. With each week that went by, I noticed something changing within me, but I couldn't describe it. I started having dreams about becoming lighter and felt a shift in the way I perceived the world. At this point, all I was certain of was how much I loved my son. Everything else in my life seemed of little importance.

Up until this time, my measure for success had been completely material. I grew up in the 1950s, in Southeast Los Angeles, where my family lived below the poverty level. Neither parent had finished grade school so there was no intellectual stimulation. There wasn't a book to be found in our house. The food stamps always ran out, leaving us without basic necessities for days. Oftentimes, my stepfather would drive my sister and me to grocery stores with an empty bag and a note which read, "Our family is starving. Please help us." We would drive from store to store until our bags were full. My earliest memories were of being hungry and wondering if there would be enough food for the next meal. By the time I was age 10, my sister and I had carved 20 notches in our headboard, each mark representing a different home we had lived in. Our family moved from one cheap, run-down house to another, usually ushered out of the last one by sheriff's deputies. There were even a few months when we lived out of my stepfather's car. No one ever came to visit us socially, nor did we have any religious exposure. Ultimately, there were nine of us living in a two-bedroom house with one bathroom.

My young life in servitude kicked into full force with the advent of the seventh child. Being the oldest, I knew no such thing as playtime. After school, my chores began: nonstop diaper changing, bottle feeding, cleaning and dishwashing. I tended to the backlog of dirty cloth diapers for hours every day. The smell was unbearable. If I dared complain, my stepdad would hit me so hard I traveled airborne across the room. This flight would end only when the barrier intercepted my body and where, seeing stars, I finally hit the ground. He would shout at me to get up and stop crying and then hit me again. I lived in a constant state of fear and terror. I quickly learned how to numb my physical body from the abuse of my stepfather. No matter how well behaved I was, he always found a reason to strike out. All I wanted to do was run as far away from these people as I could. I'd seen television shows that portrayed happy family scenarios and I longed for a life of abundance and security. This is where I split consciously and created a future dream world in my mind. A dream I clung to for survival. By living in this dream, I was able to survive the abuse. My mother seemed helpless and trapped by her circumstances. I witnessed her life being threatened several times a week by my rage-aholic stepfather. This dreadful childhood of lack, abuse and hunger was hard to let go of in my adult years. But now, suddenly, the hole in my heart was being fed with love from an innocent child—my son Michael. I was experiencing unconditional love for the very first time.

When Michael was about 4 months old, his pediatrician called. He was suspicious that there was something medically wrong with Michael. He had performed two sets of DNA tests, which confirmed that Michael had Down syndrome. The doctor said that my son would most likely die before the onset of puberty from a host of irreversible congenital abnormalities. He predicted Michael would have slow cognitive abilities and trouble speaking. He said there was no hope.

My first reaction was anger at the doctor for stating Michael's case was hopeless. At that moment while listening to the pediatrician, it was as if my life suddenly caved in. I went into a deep state of shock, but not because he had Down syndrome. I loved him no matter what. The fear of losing him and all the love that had finally arrived in my life was unbearable. The happy, healthy family I had dreamed of and worked so hard to make real was being taken away. My world was being turned completely upside down. I couldn't accept it!

For several weeks prior to this moment, outside of my life with Michael, the feelings of emptiness had progressed to a near mental breakdown. I would drive to the office and sit at my desk, staring blank faced, out my penthouse window. I could not even perform the most basic functions. I fell deeper into the shock of the new reality before me. I didn't fully realize, until now, that I had lived my entire life mentally and emotionally split from myself, living in a dream of the future that was not real. I created it in order to survive the abuse as a boy. I was still there as a man but I could no longer maintain the illusion. It all came crashing down. Weeks went by and I had still not told Rose about my condition. She had no idea what was going on inside me and this was not the time to tell her. I had completely shut down. Rose had also withdrawn into depression but we were unable to help each other.

While researching Michael's condition, I learned that no one could be sure how severe internal organ abnormalities would be in a child until the embryonic and neurological development was complete at the end of the first 12 months of life. We decided that my wife Rose would take our 6-month-old son overseas for controversial cell therapy. The trip was very expensive, and only one of us could go so my son and wife left for Europe.

CHAPTER 2

THE END OF THE AMERICAN DREAM

Still in shock, I felt something inside begin to communicate. Uncharacteristic thoughts and feelings arose as I underwent a life review that became a nonstop process, taking on a creation of its own. In those first months with Michael, my intuition began to open naturally. I received a flow of thought and feeling impressions that gently impressed themselves on my mental, emotional and feeling awareness. The gentle heart opening I had experienced with Michael showed me that a profound place of wisdom existed within me. I started paying attention to these thought and feeling impressions which were emanating from the center of me more and more. Each time I did, they would reveal a new layer of truth within me; and simultaneously reveal the emotional wounds that were covering the truth of who I really was. These emotional wounds had fragmented the wholeness and innocence of my very being. I began to passionately embrace this awareness even though I was heading into the unknown. I had to! I felt so lost. Where else could I go but within. The more I received, the more I wanted to know. I had no idea that this would mean unraveling every unhealthy emotional construct I had acquired.

Every few days, a new thought or feeling impressed itself into my day-to-day awareness with concepts such as, "You're living in the future, and sacrificing the present." This revelation about "present Frank" rang completely true. I was also becoming aware that my strong personality had been formulated out of fear to protect the wounded child within me. I was completely separated or split off from my authentic self. Outwardly, I came across as insecure, overly defensive and full of anger and resentment. I clearly had a chip on my shoulder. Out of a need to be perfect, I developed many smooth facades for every occasion or situation in life. If someone would point out and accurately describe my behavior, I would inwardly deny and immediately deflect such criticism with clever reasons for my demeanor, but I knew they were right. Why was I that way, I wondered.

In rare moments, when I would feel my authenticity, I saw that I had a deep reverence for the beauty in all things and a great wonderment to explore the world around me. I also had a strong belief that miracles were the rule and not the exception. I was very positive, loving, compassionate, enthusiastic, open minded and fearless. However, this side of me rarely showed itself as I felt buried under the burdens of the past. So much so, it felt uncomfortable to be in the joy of my authentic self. I did not know how to bridge this side of me and so I predominately lived out of my body in a future dream world I created to survive. By living in the future, I robbed myself of the joyful presence found in every "moment" of life.

It took awhile to realize that my spiritual, higher self could get through my defenses and communicate in its natural, intuitive way. With more clarity, however, I was beginning to understand that the habit of living in the future was keeping me from a better present. Even so, I did not know how to live in the day-to-day world, let alone the moment. My life looked well adjusted, but I was awash in multiple façades fueled mostly by the desire to survive.

A second recurring thought impression revealed that I was split and disassociated within myself. Being split and disassociated is a very common coping mechanism for those who have experienced childhood abuse. One persona, for example, was overly pleasing and accommodating, a developed behavioral mannerism, in order to keep me safe from my stepfather's physical rage. Another was to appear mellow and calm, self-sufficient and without expressing any personal needs in order not to provoke his rage against me. I also stuffed and repressed the anger and rage growing inside me as a result of the treatment I had received.

A third thought impression was a question: "How can true love find me if my authentic self is nowhere to be found?" This was the most devastating message, for it impacted every part of my being. Everyone wants to be loved, held and seen, appreciated and cared for. I never felt loved as a child. Rather, I felt hated. I never saw the love between a man and a woman, only violence. Childhood memories, along with feelings of despair, began to surface more frequently. I couldn't stand it! It felt as though mental and emotional patterns buried deep within were responsible for my severe mood swings. I could see the connections. I knew I was avoiding disharmony at all cost, even though I was angry toward my mother for her choices and about the way we had grown up. I also knew I carried a lot of resentment and an enormous chip on my shoulder. I did not trust people in general. Without positive role models, I could imagine only what I didn't want to become. How could I validate my manhood or be myself, for that matter? My authentic self had been lost and buried for safekeeping long ago. How would I be able to recover what was lost?

Weeks went by, yet I was so overwhelmed with grief that I was unable to work. I could no longer meet my responsibilities—to my employees, my partner, our clients or my wife for that matter. I felt frozen. I asked my business partner to buy me out. The real future had arrived, shattering my fantasy. As the here and now broke through and cracked my illusory world of escape, the full weight of reality, a world of pain, rushed in.

My wife was also in shock, and our marriage deteriorated fast. She had just given birth to our amazing and healthy daughter Mary. I was troubled by what Mary's first impressions of the world might be. Her parents were at odds, her father was having a breakdown and all attention was going to Michael. I worried that patterns of abandonment and rejection would fill her subconscious. But how could I help her? Though I was still able to function, I couldn't work. Very strange! The overwhelming drive I once had to take care of business was gone. It wasn't long before the homes and cars were returned to the bank. My wife felt betrayed, and so did I. We divorced.

I was dazed and unsure about my life. So much had happened so fast. Oddly, I felt okay about losing my business and home. It was good not to have the stress of such high personal expenditures, about $15,000 a month as I recall, a lot for a 30-year-old. My breakdown lasted for almost three months, during which time I seemed to have no control over the dramatic changes occurring in my life. I sensed something powerful moving my life's flow into another direction. I wanted my life back the way it was, and yet at the same time, my heart was leading me in a new direction. I wondered what was awaiting me.

I had lost my business, most of my possessions, my wife and my home. I had limited time with my children. It wasn't that I was helpless, but I felt strange feelings of not caring about the material structures I had built my life upon. My mind would tell me that my new direction flew in the face of logic and convention, but I was zombie-like when it came to fighting for what I had built. That life was gone.

It was obvious that the answers to my breakdown were being intuitively revealed by these thought impressions surfacing from my heart. When children experience fear, terror, emotional, mental or physical abuse, they split or fracture the energy of their consciousness in order to survive. It is like going into shock with the inability to recover. It can feel like part of you went to some far off place to escape the horrifying pain of being rejected, neglected or abused. In truth, any treatment in the absence of love is abuse. Another common defense is to mentally block out the memory of a single event or years of ongoing mistreatment, but the emotionally charged memories will eventually surface and need to be dealt with. Triggering events, such as dis-ease, loss or a physical, mental or emotional breakdown will erupt to signal that old emotional wounds can no longer be held within.

I knew I was somewhere else, but I could do nothing to bring myself back. It was eerie to be between the worlds of consciousness. I began to recognize I had multiple facades as though I was an actor on a stage becoming a different character to suit the moment or cope with life but I felt very far from myself. I could feel and see the positive qualities in me but at the same time I could feel and see the unhealthy qualities or behaviors overlaying these good qualities causing great confusion within me. These pockets of consciousness within me felt like pieces of me that were hurt and could not find their way back to the whole of me.

I was able to see the many times I had fractured myself as a boy to survive. As I looked further, I observed that my present energy was also in multiple pieces, too afraid to reunite with my adult self. I was unnerved; this must be the purpose of the breakdown. Nevertheless, I wasn't completely broken and retained enough awareness to be rational. The mind has an amazing ability to overcome severe emotional stress. Our job is to heal the subconscious and unconscious in order to be whole and happy again.

To give birth to my true self and discover who I really was, I would have to reunite the fractured pieces of my soul.

It was no accident that the strange cloud of frozen ambition began to disappear when my corporation was sold and my marriage ended. A huge force of energy from inside and out was dramatically changing the direction of my life. Strangely, I felt it was okay, even though existence as I had known it was stripped away. My spiritual nature began to reveal where I was in separation so I might choose to rediscover who I really was.

Self-judgments and beliefs about our early life separate us from who we are. But the soul is designed to awaken, unify and evolve its human consciousness through our spiritual self or the higher vibratory presence within. When it is time, soul energy begins to elevate our vibration, bringing rapid change to all mental and emotional distortions. We then have the opportunity to experience our expanded, universal soul presence or what we call God.

What and where is our soul? Our soul is golden light. To experience this light, you must go within to the center of your human beingness to the soul spark within your heart. Once you enter the soul-light within your heart, you enter the direct experience of the soul's vast and expanded levels of conscious awareness, which pervades throughout "The All There Is." Its qualities are love and a unique knowledge of being held in the light. Our bodies are the end point of the soul's light, which flows around and through us, yet in higher vibration. Our soul is part of the tremendous force of the unified field in which we co-create reality with every emotional thought. Not a moment is wasted by our soul in the guiding of our lives, especially in matters of the heart and our highest good. When we ignore our spiritual unfolding, life is uncomfortable because happiness and joy become harder and harder to find.

When our soul incarnates, as a child and a babe, we all have the same question; how will I be loved here on earth? We have just come from the light of all souls or what we call Heaven, where we are all connected to each other with love, and the light of our soul's light that streams through all of us like a unified field. It is this soul-level connectedness that gives our earthly self a powerful need to belong to each other. As a child we only want to know how we are going to be loved here. Thus, any treatment we receive we interpret as love even if it is abuse. Week by week and month by month, as we experience this abuse or neglect, we slowly experience the loss of innocence. As we enter adulthood, we expect to receive the same treatment we received as a child because that is what we learned is love. The unified field of Heaven also exists on earth. The longing within the heart of all humanity is to return to this connectedness of the unified field. What separates us from each other is judgment and placing *value upon, rather than all being equal and yet unique. Until we heal the patterns of abuse and self judgment, we will not know the true experience of love and being loved.*

CHAPTER 3

MIRACLE ON THE BEACH

As had become my ritual, I was sitting by myself on the beach one day, watching the waves and pondering what to do with the rest of my life. Suddenly, I had a most unexpected vision in which time and space seemed to alter. An adult Michael and a younger version of myself materialized right in front of me! In a flash, I was transported into the vision and the younger character, who was me. All aspects of the vision felt just as real as the reality I had been experiencing on the beach. As soon as I adjusted to what seemed like a dream, my grown-up son began to speak. I immediately felt intense love flowing from Michael into my entire body. Tears swelled in my eyes as the flow entered parts of me where love and innocence had long been lost.

He greeted me and said, "It is time to remember and awaken." I thought to myself, "Remember what?" Instantly, he answered my thought! "The world is not what it seems. The surface of life is a construct of energy—of thought forms, the conscious mental projections of collective humanity, which are mentally created and based on fear, judgment and loss. Beneath this surface reality is a world very much alive. Deeper beneath the surface, there are powerful energies within the elements of nature, and more dynamically, the inner co-creative forces within the human auric field. These energy forces are all interactive with each other. You have come to remember this and rediscover what is inside and all around you! Within your soul memory is Ancient Wisdom, the secret of the light and accessing the divine. You are of the blue ray, a messenger of God. I am here to initiate your awakening. It is time to remember why you have come, which happens when you go within. As you do, discovery of 'who you are not' is revealed, and will open the door to 'who you are.'"

I asked why I sometimes felt so sad and alone. He answered, "You feel alive, but you are separated from the energy of 'aliveness' that is everywhere around you. You must relearn how to interact with the part of you that is one with the unified field."

I asked what was separating me from this energy. He said, "Layers and layers of the dark, discolored residue of emotional wounds. When children experience hurtful or harmful moments, of which there are hundreds, they accumulate heart-breaking memories. This energy muddies and contracts the otherwise expanded and luminous human energy field. Week by week, month by month, year by year, these experiences form layers and layers of scar tissue that slowly cut off or separate the child's luminous aura from the energy of 'aliveness.' In each human, this creates a powerful longing of the heart to belong, to be loved and to reconnect with self and nature."

I asked why I felt so much love from him. He said, "Because you do not know love, yet you are love. The love deep within you recognizes the love within me and comes alive again! Like most humans, you grew up with conditional love. You were told, 'Do this; don't do that. Be like this. Don't cry. If you act in a certain way, only then will I love you.' When you were not understood as a child for being unique, it signaled some part of yourself to shut down. If a child is not held (physically or emotionally), she or he feels not lovable, not good enough. If he experiences fear and abuse, he forever tries to please, sacrificing his own essence to be loved. The child literally reshapes his auric energy field, lowering the vibration of his essence. Layers and layers of clouded energy begin to form unconscious patterns of loss and shame."

I asked how we were having this conversation. He explained, "Because I have not lost my innocence, my 'aliveness.' I am one of your teachers in this life. The other is Archangel Gabriel, the angel of hope. He inspires those who are in divine service to humanity. You are one of God's messengers, and we are having a big talk to inspire your self-discovery and healing. Then you will remember and be compelled to share your discoveries with others."

He waived his hand, seemingly to access another dimension where many lifetimes could be shown to me. He explained that we had incarnated many times together. "In every life, we have been teachers to one another, awakening the 'light of the soul' when the time was right. This life, I came to initiate and ignite your awakening to love. Your breakdown is the beginning. There is much to undo. You must heal and transmute all the contracted energy that suppresses the love and light already inside. This will take many years."

"It was your soul's desire to know divine, unconditional love while in the physical body; not just to know it, but to experience the true meaning of communion and the source of your being. When you achieve this, and you will, you will have rediscovered the secret to accessing the divine. The inner wisdom will appear in many forms as you awaken, and then you will share this with others. Yours is a great adventure. Know that your success is assured!"

Michael's image and the sound of his voice began to fade away. Was I dreaming? Had I fallen asleep? No. I had been awake the whole time. I could still hear and see the waves in the background. Wow! What did he mean by "messenger"? I had never heard of Archangel Gabriel, though I did remember the extraordinary balls of white light that visited whenever Michael and I were alone together. And I sensed the importance of his words when he spoke of initiation, finding the light within and telling others. Was this real? Our egoic minds love to question everything. How could I know for sure? I put my mind to rest; yet, I had just conversed with my son, who appeared to be about 30 years old. At the same time, I knew he was at home with his mother and was still a baby.

A few years went by after the vision with Michael. The divorce put a strain on the time I could be with him; visitations went from once a week to once a month. It was breaking my heart not to be with him in a regular family setting. My daughter Mary would sometimes have the saddest eyes, which I knew was because of me. How could she not feel abandoned and rejected by her father? I suppose that is the meaning of "the children will inherit the sins of the father." But I felt powerless to alter the course of these events. Her longing seemed an extension of my own. I did not have a father in my life while growing up either. A missing parent leaves a place of emptiness, a haunting feeling that seemingly can't be filled. What would her relationships with men be like? Would they always drop out of her life or not be emotionally available? I feared that her sadness would later manifest as anger, with rejection and aloneness at its core.

My reality now mimicked my early life, filled with the same emotions even though now I was the father. I had failed to keep everyone together. Michael was growing and doing well. After mast cell therapy in Germany, he had maintained a steady course of speech therapy and early cognitive stimulation. His mother became a teacher so that she could keep close tabs on his development. She was now his heroine. He attended school like any other child, but in special education classes. His mother saw to it that he was taught how to read. He learned quickly and has been functioning at a high level ever since. He did not suffer any of the health problems predicted by our pediatrician. He maintained a divine quality, although his early mystical communication with me began to fade. Perhaps his "mission" of initiating my awakening was complete. Whenever we were together, I felt more alive. He would joke and say, "Dad, there's that good old feeling," referring to our company of angels and the love and light all around us. Sometimes he would point to a family scenario where someone was being mistreated and say, "Dad, that's wrong-o in the Congo."

Feeling love from Michael was powerful, far beyond what I imagined was the normal father-son relationship. It overwhelmed me with joy, as if he were a living saint or angel; I had never felt this way before with anyone. Somehow I had lost, or just never experienced, such love while growing up. I wanted to understand this feeling.

Did living in fear each day of my early life color over the love within me? Michael had spoken of the layers of emotional guarding and the walls of protection we put around us. In my case, this energy was self-sabotaging. I so longed for love, yet I did not recognize it. Early on we construct our energy field to survive abuse, only to have to undo these constructs later in life to fulfill the heart! He also mentioned the "energy of aliveness" that would result from reconnecting with the self or that part of me that had experienced the loss of innocence. I wondered where love comes from and about Michael's answer, "We are love."

All people, including even those few who have started to explore their own unconscious mind and emotions, habitually overlook the strong link between the child's longing and unfulfillment and the adult's present difficulties and problems, because only very few people personally experience, and not just recognize in theory, how strong this link is. Full awareness is essential.

— Eva Pierrakos, *The Path Work of Self-Transformation*

CHAPTER 4

THE JOURNEY WITHIN

Inspired by my extraordinary vision of Michael, I began reading every spiritual book I could find with the hope of understanding what he meant about awakening and the initiation of light. I discovered an intense passion to know myself. The books I read all seemed to say that meditation and healing is the path to self-discovery. Like developing a new skill, it would require discipline and practice to find one's self. I read that as you go within— observing thoughts, feelings and emotions—a door opens that leads to your authentic being.

I worked so hard at meditation, but for months nothing happened. I figured something was wrong with me. Then, one day I just sat down by a tree and gave up trying to make it happen. My body suddenly went limp, and I felt a deep peace within, which I didn't even know was there. Wow, I thought. There are miracles inside of us that can bring relief to our lives and are just waiting to be discovered. I suppose you could say I finally surrendered. My thinking just stopped; a feeling of tranquility continued to unfold within me. I had discovered the feminine principle of allowing, which brings forth the magic of the spiritual self. I had just learned that focusing so hard with the mind on doing may limit what is possible. Let the mind go, and all will open.

Every book I read provided some insight and impact. One that really stood out, with its mystical setting of Machu Picchu in the Andes Mountains of Peru, was Shirley MacLaine's *Out on a Limb*. I was astonished that this part of the world felt so familiar to me. As I read the book, my emotional body resonated with the feeling of running from Andean peak to peak in another time, another life. I didn't know I could feel my emotional body! As I had that thought, a voice within said, *"Become interactive with your feelings."* I asked what exactly was the voice saying, and who was speaking. I didn't get a direct answer, yet I heard, *"Slow your mind, your thoughts, and feel the life force of you!"* I suspected it was Gabriel, but I wasn't sure. I followed the advice of the inner voice and was jolted into feeling the joy and excitement of what it was to be a tribal messenger. I was a pre-Incan; I ran the Andean peaks from tribe to tribe and could feel the energy of those mountains. It was amazing. That's when I realized that we carry our memories with us life after life. I dubbed this part of me the "memoric body." In my present life, I still enjoy a good run; it always feels so meditative!

The books I was drawn to read all contained truths that stirred distant memories and provided new insights. Shirley MacLaine's experiences of synchronicity, of being drawn to certain places for the specific reason of remembering, excited me beyond belief. Tales of her discovery of lovers from past lives and her out-of-body experiences with the light reminded me of something my son Michael had said: "Every life we have lived, we came to discover the light within."

Another book that inspired me and gave a direct experience of universal energy was Max Freedom Long's *Secret Science Behind Miracles*. In it, he describes the Hawaiian way of accessing "manna," the pure consciousness of creation. The Kahuna's can measure a medicine man's ability to access this universal energy. My curiosity got the best of me so I tried it on a friend. With my friend's back to me, I instructed him to stand firmly in place. I placed both open palms of my hands about six inches away from his upper back. The energy started to pull his body toward me and so I found myself shuffling backwards to keep the distance between us. To my astonishment, I "magnetically" pulled him backwards over thirty feet without ever touching his body. He said it was like being in a force field and that his feet simply shuffled as if he were weightless. I learned from Long and the Kahuna's that we can interact with the energy around us through a combination of feeling and mental focus and the intention to merge with positive universal energy. It reminded me of Michael's reference to a unified field and that we are an extension of this field.

James Redfield's *Celestine Prophecy* reached the depth of my soul and activated an instant, profound knowingness of the living truth. It spoke directly about what Michael had referred to as the "energy of aliveness" and about how everything is connected by the unified field. I was blown away. These teachings affirmed a dynamic way of living and interacting with the world. After reading the nine insights of the prophecy, my life became a feeling, experiential adventure, not an intellectual one. Most important was that the book presented a way to use one's mind, instinct, and intuition combined with feelings. After digesting the first seven insights, I realized that many of the ways of living this truth were already occurring in my life. This must have been part of what Michael meant about remembering and awakening!

Even though the dramatic changes in my life seemed to fly in the face of logic and conventional wisdom, I had a strong inner sense that I was on the right track. This was of great comfort to me. I trusted what was unfolding, what I call "faith applied," which means to have no fear and everything will be okay. *This is the way of the heart!* I kept reading those insights over and over. There were amazing parallels that helped make sense of my first few months with Michael. The insights were like a checklist for understanding the drastic inner and outer changes in my life. While working with this information, I realized that the layers over my heart Michael had pointed to were unresolved emotions from childhood traumas.

I carefully reviewed my past and remembered all the stressful times that I had lost connection with my true self. From a new spiritual perspective, I came to admire, respect and, for the first time, *love* the younger me who had endured such a difficult childhood. In fact, it was clear that these emotional wounds were showing the way to what could be an incredible path of self-discovery.

My mother was a waitress and single parent for the first four years of my life. The identity of my real father was kept a secret. All my mother would say was that he was not a good person. She was barely 17 years old when I was born. I remembered that not all the babysitters were kind. During that time, my sister came along. I was between four and five years old when my mother married my first stepfather. While she worked days and most nights, my stepfather and a friend of his were molesting my sister and me. My mother never knew anything about this activity; he threatened us and swore us to secrecy. He scared me so much that I would often wet my pants when he was home. He would discipline me for wetting, further shaming me by rubbing my nose in urine. I remember hearing my little sister's screams across the hall. Even at four years old, I felt guilty that I could not protect her. This man was in our lives for only one year, but my sister and I were forever scarred and traumatized by him.

My second stepfather was 6 feet 4 and a physically abusive rage-aholic. He was very scary, but he was not sexually abusive. Because of his anger, he was unable to hold a job for more than a month. By the time I was 15, the oldest of seven children, my first sister had already run away. His habit of punching me so hard that I'd be airborne until I hit a wall persisted all those years. One time he sent me flying through a plate glass window which shattered as my body flew through it. The impact left a gaping wound in my arm—blood, veins and bone were exposed. I could see it all. One final day, this level of brutality came to a climax, when, as he chased me down the hall, I ran into the bathroom and locked the door. As he was breaking the bathroom door down in an uncontrollable rage, an inner voice told me, *"Leave, for this time he will hit you so hard it will kill you!"* I escaped by squeezing through the tiny bathroom window. At that moment I decided I would leave and never return. I never looked back.

By this time, I was earning my own money delivering newspapers, mowing lawns and washing dishes at a local café. I knew I could take care of myself; however, minors weren't allowed to live alone. My mother called the police and they came to school and talked with me. I told them my story, and they picked up my stepfather and brought him to the station on suspicion of child abuse. I didn't know there was such a thing! I informed the police officers that I would never return to that house and live with my mother and stepfather. When this happened, my mother decided it was time to reveal the whereabouts of my real father. Up until this time, I never knew who my father was or anything about him. My mother never spoke of him but I carried a deep longing, sadness and curiosity to know who my father was and also what he looked like. How could I know what kind of man I would become without ever meeting and knowing him? It always haunted me and I felt like a part of me was missing.

I was stunned! I was so angry with her for never telling me who and where he was! How could she have allowed all these years of mistreatment by my stepfathers when she knew he lived only 45 minutes away. The police called my real father. He agreed to meet with me and decide whether to let me live with him for a while. We met the next day. Even though the longing of my heart to meet him was being fulfilled, I was full of attitude. Life had been pretty tough up until then. I hoped he would like me and ask me to come live with him. At the same time, I was pissed off and carried a big chip on my shoulder because he had been absent from my life. There he was, very good-looking, wearing a sport coat and a Hollywood smile. Immediately, he said he was glad to see me; it was my mother who had made him stay away all these years. He said I looked a lot like him, and I agreed. He said he had an extra room and would be glad to have me. He owned a large construction business and loved to water ski and ride motorcycles. He didn't mind the attitude, having grown up in similar circumstances. He briefly described how he grew up in a foster home with a disciplinarian who worked him to death and beat him regularly. It was obvious he had lived on the streets. He had a James Dean quality about him, yet he was smooth and charismatic. I told him I would have to transfer to a nearby high school. He said it was not a problem as Glendale High was less than a mile away.

My father's home was beautiful; there was a pool, cars and boats—I had never seen so much and he provided for my every need. He and Eleanor, his wife at the time, were very kind to me. The new peer group of friends I found myself with had a profound impact on me. Their fathers all held college degrees and prestigious careers within the community. I was no longer engulfed in neighborhoods with gangs, drugs and the sound of occasional bullets. Even while enjoying a weekend party, my new friends always spoke of what college and careers they were considering. Their future ambitions took center stage as opposed to getting high for some escape. This influence couldn't have come at a better time. I worked part time, finished high school and prepared to attend Glendale Junior College, and then a university. But my father wasn't a saint. He drank too much, and when he did, he became violent toward Eleanor and this horrified me! I began to see the dark side of him. He loved being a ladies' man and was well known in every restaurant in town. He would frequently take me out to the bars even though I was underage, and before long, I got caught up in his life style and began drinking and womanizing right along with him. At first all this social life was glamorous for a young man craving attention. I realized very soon, however, that I was being exposed to a rather unhealthy lifestyle. The novelty wore off as I noticed my father's masterful ability to use and exploit people. He enjoyed his dark side, and I observed others being hurt by him. I had many new friends, and I noted that their fathers and family life were much different. They all seemed to be educated, and though not perfect, they never demonstrated violence at home. As time went on, my father's charisma and facades gave way to his uneducated ignorance. He was simply a cool adolescent trickster who grew up on the streets and never finished high school. I finally discovered why my mother did not want me to know him—he had been incarcerated for armed robbery at the time of my birth. So ultimately, the more I got to know him, the more the relationship became a disappointment. My emptiness remained and I continued to long for a fatherly role model. My time with him demonstrated lessons of deceptive social behavior and masking pain and anger with drinking. He was a casebook example of what happens when men can't find a way to deal with their pain and then take it out on others. Alcohol got the better of him.

This transitional period of living in Glendale with my biological father and new peer group probably saved my life and inspired my passion for education. I felt I could do it, even though I worked full time. It took four years to finish junior college, and I then enrolled at USC. One day my long-lost sister called and said she was working at a mortgage banking firm. The building demand was so high that banks could not keep up with it. The mortgage business was booming, so I went down to investigate. Within two years, I was owner and president of Fidelity First Mortgage Corporation of Newport Beach and began living the American Dream.

Each time I reviewed my childhood, I would discover something new. I felt the inhibitions related to moments of intimacy that were rooted in shame around my own needs not being met (deep unworthiness). The effects of physical abuse, living in a large family without nurturing and not receiving enough love from my mother had taken their toll. I am mindful that there is no blame; parents simply love the best they can. But I was left as one who was needy, over pleasing and insecure. My personality was partly formed by my early environment; I was insecure and needed to control everything. I did not trust people or the world; I had lived in fear, been hit all the time and watched my mother's life threatened, instead of being embraced and protected. Even though I became successful, I had the consciousness of lack because of growing up on welfare and being forced to beg for food. I always thought that food would run out. My real self was buried so deep because my uniqueness had never been embraced or allowed to be expressed; I had learned to ignore this part of myself until it had all but disappeared. This is an example of how a child separates from his or her true self, the part that isn't loved. We are literally taught to lose our selves in order to be loved, or just survive. We take on this teaching in the form of inner beliefs, the energetic layers of emotional wounds that Michael was talking about. These acquired experiences reshape our auric energy field and darken a previously illuminated aura. Emotional traumas encapsulated with dark energy had completely shaped my inner life, even though on the outside I had many facades to mask what was on the inside. I was beginning to obtain more self-knowledge and understanding. It was incredibly helpful to know the mechanisms, the whys, even the energy of my behavior. The energy of what was held within translated to feelings that were always there—sadness, aloneness, not good enough and anger that I did my best to suppress. The inspiration of Michael's message and the insights and teachings of many spiritual books were nurturing forethought to be self-aware, to feel!

My connection to my guide, who I suspected was Archangel Gabriel, continued to grow stronger. I could tell a gentle presence was always at hand. When I was feeling down, love would well up from within. No matter what was happening, I had an inner attitude of unending hope that would fill me like a cup that runneth over. Archangel Gabriel is the angel of hope and divine messenger of communication. He is the messenger of God that spoke to Moses and Mohammed. Sometimes I would have a sudden urge to act on something—read a certain book or follow a persistent feeling impression that I had been ignoring. I often sensed a distinct nudge toward everything that would stimulate my remembering. My relationship with Archangel Gabriel was just beginning; this was just a preview of what was to come. Bringing forward an enormous volume of soul memory (such as being an Andean holy man, Native American Shaman and an Essene at the time of Christ) was about to go into warp drive. Was this part of the remembering of great earth wisdoms? I couldn't help but wonder. Where was it all going? It must be an important matter given this much attention from an archangel. Eventually he would appear in his full grandeur.

My previous life had completely broken down. I began to be with myself, to be in witness to all aspects of my being in day-to-day life—my inner beliefs, my opinions, my reactions to people, my ability to be intimate yet inhibited in a relationship, and my sensitivity to people around me. There was an obvious correlation between my personality and the memories of my past. They had a dysfunctional influence, at times self-sabotaging, even though I didn't want them to. I was beginning to know myself by embracing life with a new spiritual framework. I was ready to move on with my journey and excited about recovering the ancient wisdom that Michael had spoken of. But, as Michael had said, it would take many years before I rediscovered the true meaning of communion and the secrets to accessing the divine.

I was becoming more aware of my four bodies of existence: my mental body, physical body, emotional body, and spiritual body. By paying attention to them, they reveal what's beneath the surface, and when united, they open the door to the most amazing adventure you'll ever take—the discovery of your spiritual, mystical self, and the light of the soul. Each body has distinct energy signatures. I found that by being interactive with them, the adventure of self-discovery accelerates. By aligning all four bodies, you will unearth emotional beliefs that self-sabotage. The symbol for this is the cross, or suffering on the cross. The cross has four points. When they are aligned, the center (heart) opens and suffering ends. As a result, inner emotional wounds are revealed, chaotic behavior ends and healing begins. This isn't automatic, however. You have to want it and set your intention to manifest it!

Each of the four bodies is marvelously unique:

* * Our mental capacity receives thought impressions and directs imagination. We can manifest energy at the speed of thought and the speed of emotion, especially when thoughts and emotions are focused together.*

* * Our emotions also drive thoughts. Emotions act to inform us that something is right or not so right, guiding new thought choices.*

* * Our feeling body safeguards emotional energy of the heart. Feeling impressions are intuition from the heart and higher mind.*

* * Our physical body, our body temple, is in reverence of the miracle, always registering the joys and vitality of our inner nurturing of balance. So many people live only in the mind. We can choose to live separately within each body or learn to live within all of them in day-to-day life; by feeling our way through life. Maybe this is what Jesus meant by saying, "Know thyself."*

By being interactive with self, with the intention to know who you are, a secret unfolds. But to activate the sacred within, you must first manifest and follow the opening of the heart. In other words, the power of manifestation is to be interactive with your heart, with which you can accelerate self-discovery, then inner healing and finally transformation. Practicing being interactive with self was a flow of wonderment to me. I discovered that this helped me be in the moment, something that had once been difficult. I called these steps "practical awakening," or discovering the energy of aliveness!

The experiences and relationships you are meant to have are part of your soul design. Your parents, children, close friends, and any people with whom you share a passion for something are all soul mates that belong to your soul group on a higher level. These people—as well as your adversaries—are in your life because you made an agreement with them prior to this lifetime to support each other's spiritual growth. Indeed, every relationship and experience is an opportunity for you to grow and transform your life... In every one you will have to choose how you're going to grow from their reflection.

CHAPTER 5

A NEW LOVE

After the breakdown, I was completely broken to the point of feeling as though I wanted to start my life over again. I was penniless and without a car so I took a construction job in Palm Springs to get on my feet again. While there, I was drawn, almost pulled, to frequent the Creek Side Inn, which was a cafe in the center of town. I enjoyed dining there every chance I got because there was a waitress I felt an extreme attraction for. During one week, I went three times and made certain I sat at her station so that I could ask for her phone number. Each time I did, she emphatically stated, "I don't date my customers." However, on the third time, before I walked out, she handed me her number and said, "I think I have to make an exception for you."

The attraction was magnetic. I sensed immediately that I had known her before and was supposed to be with her. She was the most beautiful woman I had ever met. Dee was half French and half Greek; she had a genius IQ and played the cello. I fell deeply in love with her. Within six months, we were married and our first child was on the way. Whenever I looked at her, I couldn't understand why this amazing woman would want to be with me. Even with all the self-discovery I'd completed, I still had deep-seeded issues of unworthiness and insecurity when it came to being in a romantic relationship.

The banking business wasn't right for me, but I decided to resurrect my old career to impress her. It had come so naturally before—I could do the job in my sleep. I opened one, two, even three different branches for what appeared to be very large and stable mortgage banking firms. For each branch, I quickly generated tens of thousands of dollars in commissions only to suddenly and without warning discover the home office had been shut down by federal governing agencies, therefore cancelling the funding of loans and commissions for each branch. This was the late 1980s during the big savings and loan debacle. I endured this roller coaster of success and failure three times in one year. Unbelievable! I would pick a reputable mortgage bank, start a branch and build up huge commissions; then a government agency would close them down—all my hard work and effort wasted. Newspaper articles about each bank reported their shocking demise and the scandalous fallout. Seemingly, there were greater forces at work here. Each step of the way I convinced Dee that everything was fine and that she could trust me, but then it would happen again.

At this point, her faith and attitude began to change. She suspected I was being untruthful with my promises of a happy and secure life. Her loving attitude and intimate affection slipped away; her disappointment was palpable. I felt betrayed that she did not believe in me or, worse yet, that she could fall out of love. Nothing was ever the same again for us. I was crushed! Her withdrawal from our relationship activated my feelings of not being good enough. My fantasy of the perfect happy family was falling apart again. What happened to "United we stand, divided we fall?"

A year went by. Finally, after a lot of communication and digging, the truth emerged. She explained that she felt betrayed and could not find her way back to how she felt in the beginning of our relationship. In her "story of early life," her father had enrolled her in prestigious private schools which she loved—only to take her out again and again as finances grew tight. She felt unsafe with the constant starting and stopping and believed he never kept his promises. In addition, her father would host wild parties with drugs, where she experienced sexual abuse which complicated her feelings of betrayal and distrust. You might as well have painted her father's face over mine. From my life experience and a spiritual perspective,

I knew that I had triggered these painful emotional memories so she could choose to heal them. But would the price be the breakdown of our marriage?

That's what soul mates do for each other. The painful memories that inhibit the heart are brought to the surface of awareness, so the burdens of the past can be resolved. Soul mates also reflect to each other their amazing soul's uniqueness that has been held back, denied or suppressed. The law of attraction and the law of opposites are very much at work in this type of relationship. Whether our soul mate is a friend or a lover, the truth within us is reflected. It is the blessing and opportunity that soul mates bring to each other, so the love within is no longer held back.

The capacity to love and be loved is the longing of the heart that is common to all. It's what the soul wants in every relationship—to see the beauty and love within. You must be open minded, hopeful and willing to "know thyself" and embrace the other person. It takes two, however; and if you refuse to embrace what is before you, you will simply attract another with the same reflection. To close yourself off from giving and receiving love is to suffer and remain in the longing of love, never fully participating in the real thing. For some people, the fear, pain and mistrust are stronger than their faith in something better and the courage to change.

My beautiful wife Dee shut her emotional body down and was just going through the motions with me. The emptiness I felt after losing the experience of her love was devastating. We now had two beautiful children, but our perfect family was broken. I felt like a failure. Why was the attraction so great if it was doomed to fail? My intuition told me that the picture must be much bigger. Perhaps love and the rejection of love from another lifetime were showing up in this life—something in the causal body of the soul, unfinished business. I needed answers!

I was reading the newspaper one day and came across an article about psychic channeling. I had never been to a psychic before, and I didn't know what channeling was. The newspaper told the tale of a retired, well-to-do local couple who claimed to have been contacted by a celestial being. Mrs. Roman Villa was enjoying a comfortable and happy retirement when one day she spontaneously began to channel divine messages. It took a couple of months for her to get accustomed to "Tahar," a master from the White Lodge of Sirius. Mrs. Villa's psychic insights had proved to be remarkable. The article reported that she had the ability to read whoever was before her with incredible accuracy. That's all I needed to hear. My life had turned upside down for the second time, and it was increasingly obvious that a great force was directing me. I needed to know for certain. Was it God? Was it Archangel Gabriel? I wanted details.

I phoned directory assistance and found that Mrs. Villa was listed. Determined, I called immediately. To my surprise she answered. I told her I had read the article and wondered if I could come for a reading; I had a lot of questions. She said, "Hold just a moment please." I could hear her in the background asking someone, "Is he one of the ones who is supposed to be here?" That was ominous, I thought, but I didn't care. She came back on the line and said, "Yes, we meet on Wednesday night. Please come." I couldn't wait; maybe now I would find out what was going on with my life.

I arrived at a beautiful home and was greeted by Mr. Villa, who seemed very nice. He directed me to the living room area where eleven people already sat waiting for Mrs. Villa to begin the session. Each person in the room looked somewhat affluent and was well dressed. Mrs. Villa settled in and explained a little about the channeling process. She explained that Tahar was a masculine being and that his channeled voice would be deeper than hers. I had many questions to ask, but I didn't want to go first. I wanted to observe the others first. The visitors asked all types of questions—including many personal ones about relationships, careers, past lives, finances, spirituality, life changes and energy phenomena. The room began to fill with a sense of peace and calmness that was wonderful. Mrs. Villa appeared very calm and still in her body language. I was amazed at the speed at which the answers came. Still, I was skeptical, but when it was my turn, something extraordinary happened. As if he could read in my mind that I was doubtful about this channeling and whether it was real, Tahar began to speak to me before I could even get my question out. "Greetings divine one, we know why you are here; in fact I, we, played a part in getting you here!" Mrs. Villa was no longer sitting still and peaceful, rather she was stirring and her voice deepened while powerful energies filled the room. I could feel the hair rising on my arms and neck and positive energy filling my body. It felt powerful and wonderful!

Mrs. Villa/Tahar moved toward me and said, "You and I are old friends from another world. I have come to ease your mind with a greater understanding of what is occurring in your life." Energy from Tahar continued to flow through my entire body. A feeling of deep peace instantly relieved my anxiety. There was a gasp of surprise from the others in the group. Projecting his energy into Mrs. Villa, Tahar began moving her body slowly as if she were an ancient relic. Enveloped in her form, he sat down beside me. "You have been put through the fires recently. Your life will never be the same, and you cannot go back no matter how hard you try! You have not come to live an ordinary life. You have come with great importance."

Again, before I could ask my questions he answered, literally reading my mind. How was he doing that? "You are one of God's messengers; you are among many sent directly by God. It is important now to remember who you are." I wondered to myself, okay who am I then? Yet before I could open my mouth, he stated, "It cannot be revealed yet! It must be your decision to remember."

Oh, like I have a choice given recent events. I had just lost what I thought to be the American dream and my second marriage was failing. Tahar continued, "As to your mate, she has decided not to open to her spirituality. The pain of betrayal and being violated by her father were too great for her to overcome. You, on the other hand, have decided! It began when you allowed the love to flow into your heart, the love from your son, Michael." I was stunned! How the hell did he know about that? "I know a great many things about you; **you are the bringer of light!**"

I finally got a spoken word in. "What do you mean by that?" He answered, "You and many like you have been bringing light into the worlds for eons. You are a way shower." How does one bring the light I wondered? Immediately, he read my mind. "First you must enter the light. This is not an intellectual pursuit; it must be experienced."

With these words, an energy filled me—the energy of truth. At least that's what it felt like. A certainty rose up within me, along with volumes of other details just beyond my mental reach but close enough to feel this knowledge was there. The presence of such knowingness brought me instant peace, so much so that I forgot the rest of my questions.

He continued, "Your soul memories will stir awareness of the truth of who you truly are, slowly at first and then quickening. It must be done in this way. Then when you least expect it, the initiations of light will begin. This healing is also known as the passage into light. You must heal the past, what is known as man's inhumanity to man. In your remembering, you will rediscover the sacred arts. These are intimate ways of using the heart and mind within the body temple to access the divine."

Tears began to flow. I could feel not only this energy of truth but also of love, which began filling my heart just like when I was with Michael. "The feeling of love is undeniable when confirming the truth." Tahar shifted his energy now to give me important information. "It feels as if your children will be going out of your life and that you are powerless to prevent it; the guilt is killing you.

They are going away, but they will be in your life later. Let it go; it will not serve you. They know on a spiritual level you are here to do something important."

Then Tahar turned his attention to my relationship with Dee. "Your current marriage is a karmic one. Both of you have unfinished business from a previous lifetime. When soul mates meet, it is an opportunity to resolve previous betrayals. The love from your heart is igniting an old wound that makes her want to push love away. Her withdrawal has brought up the memories of distrust, insecurity, pain and rejection within both of you. This is the same experience you had with Michael. When his love entered your heart, it flowed into the emotional core wound where you had become separate from yourself, where you pushed love away. This resulted in your breakdown, so you could see and feel the truth within! You have chosen to heal. In her case she has chosen not to."

Oh great, I thought to myself. I wanted answers and I was getting them, but they were not what I had expected. I could feel the truth of what he was saying, but I didn't want to believe it. I was grateful for all the divine messages, especially about Dee. They were interesting, even if a bit fantastic, and hauntingly similar to Michael's. Just the same, I was in love and didn't want to let go! I still was of the opinion that I could find a solution. It was also unsettling to hear that my mortgage days were over. What on earth would I do for a living? If I were to be a bringer of the light and divine messenger, what could I possibly share? I didn't know how to heal myself or anyone else for that matter. I was bouncing back and forth between the heartbreak of real life, angelic influence whispering in my ear and an ongoing passion for new spiritual connection!

I refused to give up on my marriage and family. For months, every chance I would get, we discussed issues of the past and how they were affecting our life now. We were not happy. My feelings of insecurity and unworthiness along with her withdrawal and coldness just kept feeding each other. I was sure that with my loving support, all we needed was for her to address and forgive her childhood traumas, as I was actively addressing mine. We could heal this for our children's sake! Usually people do not know what is driving their behavior as we did. Unfortunately, as time went on, we made no progress. She listened but did not connect, yet I was relentless.

Months went by and then one day, she shocked me with her proclamation of defeat. She blurted out, "I've just given up on life. I am only here to raise the children. That's all I have to give!" I was mortified; I'd never heard such a thing! Why, how could someone enter such defeat? Her unconscious feelings had finally risen to the surface. Tahar was right! I didn't know what to do next. I couldn't just walk away. I was such a Mr. Mom. I loved cooking and caring for my children. I couldn't leave my beautiful children. Was I going crazy? Could it be happening again?

I passionately continued my course of self-discovery, hoping to make sense of it all. I read every spiritual book I came across trying to understand what Tahar and Michael had meant by remembering, healing, awakening and the energy of aliveness. I was in agony! I wanted to find out more about initiations of light. Whenever I thought of such experiences, I felt an inner energy that was exhilarating and seemed to say, "Pay attention!" Many books spoke of discovering the inner self through meditation, but I didn't find anything about initiations of light. I read stories of accessing deep levels of inner peace that could be maintained no matter what was going on around you, but that might be boring. Many claimed that meditation was the best way to hear the truth inside, but I was not convinced. I couldn't even find a concise explanation of what exactly meditation is. Maybe it's one of those things that must to be experienced to be understood, I thought.

I tried yoga, which means union. I quickly experienced yoga's ability to bring the body in union with the mind. The power to focus with intention certainly was one of the key mechanisms to the inner door! It was dramatic for me to feel so peaceful and present in my body. I enjoyed the newfound balance. It made me wonder where I had been my whole life! Yoga and breath work brought a satisfying clarity, calm and connectedness, but I sensed there was so much more. My thought impressions came from an intuitive voice deep within. With the practice of yoga, I began to feel closer to the warmth of my inner guide—a very physical sense of grounding that was unfamiliar, yet incredibly welcomed as I enjoyed a new harmony with my physical self. I sensed him just beyond an inner door, confirming what was possible.

I thought about the message that had been impressing itself upon me—the idea that I was very far from myself, the fact that I was out of my body. It occurred to me that the true self can be experienced only in the present moment. To know the truth, one must feel, not think. As Michael said, "We are Love." Well, okay then, let's go! I decided to be more disciplined. If day by day I could maintain the forethought to be within my true self, to hold a feeling of profound awareness, then maybe that door would open. I wondered what stood between the personality of my mind and the doorway to the greater self. What would I experience once I walked through that door? The scientist in me wanted to know through direct experience what all these new concepts were about.

Intimate partners provide the best reflection of where each is disconnected, inhibited or held back from love, and what each is not connected to deep within. To heal, it takes two—each needing to be open, accepting and embracing of the other and taking self-responsibility and self-accountability. My marriage to Dee revealed my tendencies to feel unworthy, insecure, not good enough and discontent with the moment. As a result, I longed for the higher attributes of the heart that bring joy, passion and fulfillment: self-love, authenticity, vulnerability, truthfulness, honoring, respect, loving and nurturing.

Why was her reaction to me so powerful? My quest within the humanity of day-to-day life began to break open the truth of discovering who I was not, revealing more about who I was. This brought a new alignment within my mental and emotional body—a way of being that opened a wide door to my spiritual nature. This type of breakthrough could happen to anyone. How? Because it is this state of allowing, embracing, observing (as we go) and accepting of the inner and outer self that paves the way to self-discovery. The process is beyond belief. The heart begins to unlock the wonders within us, demonstrating a new way of living.

So how do we get there? By recognizing ourselves in others, by identifying the emotional burdens in our subconscious and unconscious mind and, finally, by transmuting the energy of the emotional burdens we carry. Those whom we meet who greatly impact our lives are almost certainly soul mates. Can you receive the gifts they are bringing? Do you love yourself enough to embrace that which is right in front of you? There is always a teaching and reflection from which to learn. If you have eyes to see and ears to hear, you will observe it and feel it within you. Attributes of your personality, strengths and weaknesses, the energetic force of your emotions—known and unknown—that drive the out-picturing of your behavior are brought to the surface. You are offered the choice to change or to remain the same.

CHAPTER 6

BIRTH OF A HEALER

One day, I sat down by a beautiful redwood tree to meditate. I opened my eyes and thought I had been in a brief daydream, but then I realized an hour had gone by! Wow, it had finally happened! My thoughts had slowed to a full stop. When your mind stops, time shifts. In the natural letting go, the peace that is already there may overcome you. I was pleasantly overwhelmed. I wasn't used to feeling such a freedom and relief from the stresses of life. My physical body was completely relaxed as I continued to sit by the majestic redwood. If I listened hard enough, it seemed it would tell me the histories of earth. I relished the grandeur of this tree and wondered where my life was going. I didn't realize it, but my inquiry imposed a question to my higher self.

I brought myself again to a gentle place of focused allowing with the hope of re-entering that lucid space. I wanted to see if I could repeat what had just happened. In a flash, I opened my eyes with the strangest feeling. I now knew, somehow, what was going to happen next. I became interactive with my intuitive self, asking questions and getting answers. I received an intense thought impression. "It's time to become a doctor."

When I looked at my watch, I gulped. Two hours had gone by. A doctor—was I hearing things? Could that be right? I felt fantastic and energized, even happy, but what's this idea about becoming a doctor? As I thought about it, I became even more excited. Why not? I felt euphoria, completely dismissing from my logical mind the fact that no one in my family had even finished high school. It barely occurred to me that I was 36 years old and medical school would be expensive. I felt so great that I didn't care! I was motivated by the idea that such a grandiose career would inspire my wife and invigorate our marriage.

I immediately began to research all requirements to enter medical school and discovered they varied depending on specialty. The challenge of meeting the requirements grew increasingly exciting. I already had three and a half years of college in business, finance and marketing, but I was short in the sciences. I needed to attend courses in organic chemistry, anatomy and calculus, and one full year of physics. An MD degree required eight more years and at age 36, I was not happy about this. Surgery and pharmacology were not the branches of medicine I wanted to practice. Prescribing medications all day was not my idea of health care. Chiropractic was a noninvasive practice, and the medical training included three times the neurology and two full years of nutrition. I realized I'd prefer to interact with clients who were interested in helping themselves with natural, holistic and preventative methods. I doubled up on my course schedules at two junior colleges, attending both at the same time in order to finish before the next accelerated program at

Southern California University of Health Sciences. SCU's accelerated program would take three and half years with year-round classes. This meant very short breaks in-between semesters and attending 90 units of instruction per year—a grueling pace.

It all came together as if by magic. I was approved for student loans. Dee got a great job waitressing in the evenings. Knowing it was short-term, she didn't mind. After all, when I was done with my studies, she'd be married to a doctor and could be absolutely assured of a comfortable future.

I was running on raw passion and enthusiasm, a character flaw in some areas of my life, but a great strength in others. My whole life was filled with challenges, yet I was never short on positive attitude and enthusiasm. This was a powerful force within me, even through childhood. I never thought it meant much having these qualities because they felt so natural to me. Yet somehow, I became equipped with exactly what I would need to get through the life that seemed preordained for me. I always felt deep excitement, unbridled enthusiasm and a powerful acceptance that anything and everything was possible. Even while experiencing abuse, I knew there was something great watching over me and that miracles are the rule, not the exception.

I entered the enormous challenge of an accelerated medical program without any thought of the rigors. I was literally floating on positive energy and the excitement of learning how to help others. I discovered a great love for science, neurology, nutrition, natural remedies and the endless wonder that is the human body. Every day

I was on the edge of my seat so eager to learn. The first two years of the accelerated program were intense; each day I attended eight hours of lecture and labs, then studied late into the night, slept a few hours and then awakened to repeat the process. I became accustomed to the pace.

During technique lab we were required to practice on each other and I began to notice an energy healing ability emerging. In addition to chiropractic protocols, we also mastered an array of alternative techniques. All my classmates got excited when one of us would acquire a new physical symptom. We wanted to learn firsthand how effective the various treatment techniques would be. We became thoroughly familiar with each other's medical history as well as healing style. It became clear to all of us that I brought something unique to each patient encounter. When I worked on clients, they reported feeling energy moving through their body. I found this odd because I was not performing any special technique or therapy. I was focused on finding the underlying cause of each person's physical symptom. My clients always said they felt better, but I didn't know exactly why.

Little Crow

One morning I was at Dietrich's, my favorite coffee house, preparing for a final when one of the early morning regulars came over and sat beside me. It was about 5:30 a.m. and I was already into my third double espresso, getting a jump on the day. I asked what had brought him there so early. He said he delivered an early morning paper route and he was coming in for his morning cup of coffee. He said he was inspired to sit beside me to share something. He showed me a flyer about a nearby Native American church and reiterated that he felt compelled to tell me about it. He felt it might be something of interest to me.

The group was more of a gathering than a church, and the people who attended usually had an affinity to Native American religion and culture. He explained that Little Crow, a Lakota Sioux elder, was the leader. Wow, I thought to myself, how did he know? For as far back as I could remember, I've loved bows and arrows, feathers, arrowheads and especially movie scenes with ceremonial dancing. But it was more than that—all things Native American would stir the "wilds" within me. I thanked him and assured him that I was interested and would check it out.

I attended the church many times. I liked it and felt at peace there as the people were down-to-earth and without pretense. When Little Crow spoke every word seemed to touch a deep part of me. He spoke of the "old way," how every step upon the earth holds great reverence and the importance of honoring and respecting the earth. He said the old ways had become lost from modern life, contributing to a great separation between Nature and our Humanity.

Earth is the Great Mother, a sentient being. The Great Mother speaks to us, but we must learn how to listen to the wind. By feeling her rhythm, many solutions to life will be shown. The earth gives us everything we need: food, water and the air we breathe. Her body is made of the same elements as our physical body; we are the same. Little Crow spoke of the four directions of existence, of the changing rhythms and seasons in nature. Her spirit and ours are linked, not separate. Everyone and everything is connected; everything is sacred.

In the Native American culture, if one person was troubled, it would affect everyone in the tribe or community. The people supported each other and remained connected because of this belief. Each had a responsibility to be mindful of every thought, act, and deed for it would affect the next seven generations. Part of the weekly gathering was devoted to a pipe ceremony of universal prayer—for family, elders, the infirm as well as for individuals.

The Pipe Ceremony

They called it "The Gathering." Each Sunday morning after all were assembled Little Crow, acting as a tribal elder, would deliver a message about our humanity. When he was done he reminded us all that everything was sacred and that we were all connected as one. He further asked us to bring our prayers into that oneness and we would begin the pipe ceremony. I loved this part of the ceremony because it felt as though heaven and earth were moving within me. It was as if everyone that came to the gathering suddenly came into union or one body. At this moment six men quietly began a procession to the front of the room. When they reached the front of the room, they sat side by side and unsheathed their sacred pipe of peace. They filled their pipes with tobacco and began to puff on the smoke. All in attendance knew their burdens and prayers would flow up through the smoke and meet Great Spirit. However, the smoke was symbolic as the powerful energy of these prayers and burdens were flowing through the bodies of the pipe carriers. It was very powerful to witness this ceremony for you could feel the energy of Great Spirit flowing through all in attendance. The power of the Native American belief resides in the community coming together as one.

To become a pipe carrier, one had to pass many initiations and trial by fire. Few were selected for this position, which required that one needed to bear the weight of collective prayer passing through the body. In other words, the energy of the collective burden seeking relief would flow through the pipe carrier as a holy vessel on earth. A carrier typically would have been a holy man or medicine man in many past lifetimes, someone who possessed the heart and soul memory of divine service. Great focus, responsibility and reverence to God, or Great Spirit, were required.

Little Crow received visions from Great Spirit specifying who was an acceptable candidate for the honor and position of pipe carrier. He approached me after I had attended for several weeks, somewhat disturbed to report that he had received a vision that I was a pipe carrier. I believe he was concerned about how this might affect those who had observed the other carriers complete their many trials and initiations to earn the pipe carrier responsibility. I was moved to the core of my being. It was awkward, but I felt I could not refuse. It was also a stretch of Little Crow's trust and faith because this revelation was very unusual.

That Sunday, I joined the upper circle of pipe carriers in front of the gathering. The invocation of Great Spirit began. The smells of sage, sweet grass and tobacco were in the air as Little Crow and the people prayed. Tremendous energy began to flow through my body from above and below. I could feel the weight of the prayers, the longing of people's hearts—their sadness, despair, grief and loss as well as their hope. It was at this moment that my own visions and soul memories began! I was comfortable in my body, yet my awareness had become universal; the energy of my auric field was expanding in a way I had not felt before.

Memories of other lifetimes throughout the Pacific Northwest, where I had lived before as a Native American, surfaced with the intense focus on Great Spirit. I saw five lives in particular—once as a holy man, once as a medicine man, and three times as a shaman and healer. I kept hearing a phrase in another dialect over and over; finally, I received its meaning: "He who walks with the Holy Spirit; he who walks between the worlds." The images of all five beings sat together in a circle around a fire, as if they were in council. What were they contemplating, or should I say who? As soon as I observed this, they responded, "We are in council for you are awakening to the ancient wisdom within you." What wisdom? I thought to myself. They answered, "The ways of Heaven and Earth."

I realized this was becoming interactive and so I continued to mentally dialogue and ask questions. Will we be able to continue communicating like this? Are you what many people refer to as spiritual guides? "Yes, we will be communicating, and we are more than guides. We are aspects of you, held within your soul memory. Each of us (you) mastered the old ways of healing by accessing Great Spirit directly—as the spiritual essence or vibrational energy of the plant and animal kingdom, the elementals and great Mother Earth! The elementals look like white starlight or huge translucent beings that flow through the creational templates of all that is in nature. In the ancient ways, we learned how to flow and merge through multidimensional worlds. We communed with the spiritual essence of all things, which is what the Bible calls 'communion.' We call this walking in the beauty way."

"The shamans and medicine men of old knew how to expand their auric energy to merge with another human, but first they had to purify their vessel. While merging in an altered state or expanded energy presence, they would invoke God. This presence would come in the form of healing energy, the energy of light and love that transmutes every burden. You can refer to us as the council; we are here for you until you no longer need us."

The pipe ceremony was nearly complete; the memories of other times were so thick in my feeling body that it felt like I still had long hair and was wearing deerskins and moccasin boots. I remembered feeling so free and fearless, the comfort of being so peaceful and connected to everything, of being able to merge with nature. I wondered if that were possible in modern day life. Maybe this was the reason to remember and awaken—to become a healer. I could hear the council whispering, "In part that is true, but revealing divine truth can also heal collective humanity." Oh my God! What could the council mean by that? They were silent.

After the pipe ceremony, the people gathered in a healing circle. On this day, there were 150 in attendance. All those wanting a special healing for any reason placed themselves in the center. The circle formed. Everyone was hand-in-hand in a prayerful state, but now filled with a heartfelt intention to heal. The circle was so large that it went out one door and back inside the other. I was in the midst of the circle and began experiencing intense light and electric energy flowing through everyone. I felt firsthand the power of love and healing energy in the hearts of each person as it flowed from the hearts of each person in a beautiful dance of giving and receiving. Everyone within the circle was also lifting burdens, but the power of the people transmuted the heavier energies of individual burdens. The momentum of their heartful combined energy lifted the individual burdens.

It was at this point I discovered the most important aspect of my journey of awakening. Suddenly I began to feel chest pain, which became so strong it knocked me to my knees! It felt like a severe heart attack and I didn't understand why. I heard the council gently whisper, "You were taking on the pain of the people without receiving and allowing your own pain to release. You don't know how to receive healing energies due to your feelings of rejection, unworthiness and many other core emotional wounds. It is easier for you to receive for the people than for yourself. This is one of the first of many emotional burdens you are carrying that you will come to know and eventually heal—what is called purifying your vessel."

"The emotional wounds of humanity are held within memory. The energy within these memories manifests as layer upon layer of dark, low vibratory energy. These layers of energy inhibit the natural luminescence of the human auric energy field. To purify the vessel or clear these energies, one must first have knowledge, then understanding, and then healing and transmutation. This will restore the higher vibrational light within you." I found myself on my knees feeling the heaviness of the circle. People became concerned and asked if I was okay. No one around me knew of my powerful lesson about receiving. The council continued to speak.

"People of your time are conditioned to give rather than receive—a tragedy among humanity. Your people are taught the ways of fear rather than trust. This is man's inhumanity to man, and it begins in the story of early life." It took me all day to recover and get my natural vitality back. That was a heavy dose of remembering and all I could take for the time being.

There was a men's circle the following day: the Circle of Truth. The theme was a man's responsibility and accountability in relationships. What is your story of early life? Do you act with respect? Do you respect yourself? How do you treat your wife or girlfriend? How do you feel about her? How do you feel about your mother? These were the questions we were to ponder before joining the Circle. We were to come and share the truth among men, without the fear of judgment. I was excited to attend. As a young man, I didn't have an opportunity to share an experience like this with other men. There were about 30 men in the circle, and we took turns passing the talking stick. In Native American ceremony, he who holds the staff of truth must only speak truthfully, and only from the heart, during his time of sharing.

I began to contemplate the questions for the Circle of Truth. My life of mistreatment flashed through my mind. It felt so painful to think about it. I began feeling embarrassed at the thought of describing so many awful experiences. Feelings of rejection and abandonment brought tears to my eyes as I remembered growing up not knowing my real father and why he left us. Even though much later in life I would meet him, he was a profound disappointment. I still held deep resentment and anger toward my mother. Why? I was pondering how my wife and I treated each other and my predominant question to my wife was consistently, "Why, why?" "Why were you so loving at the beginning of our marriage and are now withdrawn?" I was never physically violent, but due to her withdrawal, I found myself raising my voice a lot out of frustration. I recognized this was also a form of violence.

I was last to receive the talking stick. I listened to the other men and their stories. There was a common theme of dysfunction and abuse of every variety in their everyday relationships. Each pain was some kind of extension of "the story of their early life." The treatment of the woman in their life was always a repeat of the abuse they had witnessed in their early family—men abusing women, and women abusing men. "The children inherit the sins of the father," and so it goes: Man's inhumanity to man. Their stories of adoption, drug addiction, torture, homelessness, jail and sexual abuse shocked me. They just looked like rough-edged guys to me, but listening to their stories of loss and grief was so sad and compelling that I could feel the aura of compassion thickening around us. My life story paled in comparison to theirs. I was almost embarrassed to tell mine. I had always felt so alone, but as it turns out, I am not. There are so many who are suffering. How did the world get this way? Our capacity for suffering may be enormous, but our capacity for love is greater!

My past, my mystical self and my present-day life were all colliding for a reason! The past, present and future were becoming real worlds or dimensions of existence to me—each one was influencing the others. They had feelings, energy; each dimension was alive or dead depending on my focus. My journey within continued and each time I connected the dots to my past, my self-awareness expanded. I kept feeling bigger, vibrationally more expanded and more alive, yet I also felt the presence of deeper pain waiting to express itself.

I remember Michael talking about the energy of aliveness. When you begin to connect beneath the surface of mental defenses, your authentic self begins to reveal itself. Self-discovery of where you've separated from self during emotional wounding enables you to become whole again. I came away from the Circle of Truth with a whole new perspective. I felt great. Maybe now my wife and I could find a way to grow back together.

My visit to the Circle of Truth helped me realize I was repeating the same pattern, role and relationship with my wife that I had with my mother. My relationship with my mother was filled with rejection and pain. She was beautiful and loving but not emotionally available—a haunting description of my marriage.

Receiving love in adult life requires the familiar sense of receiving love in the "story of early life." When love is absent early on, we build an aura of defensive energy around us. As an adult, when real affection and unconditional loving emotion come, it brings up the pain of hurt that we experienced as a child. We end up pushing that person away to avoid being hurt. Why? Loving energy from another is naturally healing. The first step toward emotional healing is to feel the original hurt. If we resist and stuff the pain rather than experience it for what it is, we will have to wait until it happens again. Most people are accomplished at stuffing, denying any feeling of emotional pain. This can go on for decades if we don't make the connection.

It became abundantly clear why I had been guided to the "Circle of Truth." Deeply examining your role in life—through relationships, beliefs and dysfunctional identities—is the best way to know thyself, so you can chose differently. If you have no example, no role model, it's up to you to find ways to connect to yourself. You will need to examine your actions, become accountable and take responsibility. No one can do it for you.

CHAPTER 7

MIND-BODY-SPIRIT

The New Paradigm of Healing

My studies at Southern California University provided an outstanding framework for understanding human health and healing. I was surprised to discover the connection between thoughts and emotions and our level of stress, which in turn affects our neurophysiology—the vitality and quality of life. The mind-body-spirit link is governed by thoughts and emotions. That is, the energy of what we think and feel runs directly to the mid-brain and throughout our nervous and endocrine systems. Where thoughts and emotions go, ENERGY flows. We're in charge!

The energy we generate with thoughts and emotions illuminates physical vitality or fuels fatigue, depression, anxiety and illness. Most thoughts and feelings are internalized negative self-judgment. We fill ourselves with self-doubt, condemnation and worry that we're not good enough, not pretty enough, not smart enough and so forth. Therefore, we are manifesting at the speed of emotional thought. As defined by the law of attraction, our manifest reality (and our physicality and nonphysical reality) is simply the way we are moving ENERGY! When we focus on positive thoughts we bring more happiness, joy and positivity into our lives. When we focus on the negative, we bring more negativity into our lives. In other words, we are our own self-fulfilling prophesy in wherever we direct our focus, intention or thoughts. Typically, dis-ease and physical symptoms can be associated with major life changes or chronic self-sabotaging behaviors. These symptoms provide the evidence of self-fulfilling manifested reality. Internalized stress, for example, first manifests subclinical conditions such as fatigue, a tendency toward illness, anxiety, allergies, blood sugar problems, high blood pressure and heart stress. The chronic behavior of negative internal thought conversations—obsessing over something you believe about yourself—is sourced in long-standing, subconscious emotional wounds. One really must "know thyself" to ensure a healthy energy flow.

While in school, we became good at diagnosing the multi-causal relationships of various physical symptoms and exposing their mind-body-emotion connections. Mental states, emotional conditions, diet and environment all influence the body's neurophysiology, or state of well-being. As a result, out of balance states depress our immune and endocrine systems. Too much stress, for example, precipitates an adrenal "fight or flight" response, which takes priority within the body. The average person in prolonged states of stress may notice increased fatigue, allergies, asthma, mood swings, hyper or hypoglycemia or thyroid subclinical conditions that sap the body's vitality. In class, we noticed the familiar patterning of emotional components in each patient's history. Preceding the physical symptom, we would usually find the presence of unhappiness, needs not being met, moving of one's residence, career change, divorce or ongoing drama in relationships.

Another out of balance condition is a diet deficient in minerals, protein, fiber and fruits and vegetables, which can deplete the essential nutrient stores within the body and set the stage for dysfunction. With the addition of mental and emotional stress, the right conditions exist for physical symptoms to appear. Iodine depletion, for instance, can lead to subclinical hyper or hypothyroidism, which causes hyperactivity, attention deficit and an increase or decrease in metabolism. This cascading activity severely impacts one's vitality, leading to headaches, fatigue, osteopenia and susceptibility to colds and flu. Likewise, a molecule of iron sits at the center of every red blood cell. If iron stores are depleted, resulting anemia can lead to seemingly unsolvable common symptoms in day-to-day life, such as headaches, body aches, stiffness and low energy, to name a few.

In the book *Empty Harvest*, Dr. Bernard Jensen described how food can look nutritious and yet be deficient in vitamins and minerals. This occurs partly because of improper growing methods, such as over-nitrating with chemical fertilizers and repeatedly planting the same vegetable in the same field. In the 1930s, overgrowing of this type destroyed the topsoil in the Midwest, creating the great Dust Bowl. To assure nutritious crops, Native Americans grew squash, beans and corn in the same field with good effect. One crop naturally put nitrogen back in the earth while the other was taking it out, maintaining healthy mineralized soil—and health. Today, we have even greater threats to the quality of our food, such as strong agribusiness interests, vanishing seed sources, GMO experimentation, multiple food additives and preservatives, tainted water supplies and countless health and safety codes that greatly impact the quality of foods we consume. In other words, the carrot or apple may look great but the minerals and vitamins are severely depleted. While you may be eating from the four food groups each day; unfortunately, your body may not be receiving the vitamins and minerals it needs. Over time, this results in a chronic state of malnutrition and physical symptoms that seem to appear from nowhere.

People tend to internalize emotional stress in certain organs, meridians and chakras of the body. The possibility of increased dis-ease after prolonged stress is predictable. Stressful life conditions are nearly always driven by deep unconscious emotional wounds from childhood. The body and mind remember every single moment of your life. When we choose not to connect to what is deep within, the energy from our wounds collects around an organ, gland or part of the body with a genetic predisposition to be weak. A deep emotional wound, coupled with a great intensity to repress and deny, will result in chronic or acute physical symptoms—the stronger the pattern, the more severe the dis-ease.

Hereditary or genetic predispositions for dis-ease are linked to parents who did not get in touch with their emotional wounds and thereby have perpetuated a family life that demonstrates the dramas of childhood. This is how patterns are set up physically through familial histories and passed on to the children: "The sins of the father are inherited by the children," as the saying goes. The good news is that a genetic predisposition need not express itself. What can really improve your life, vitality and health is to make peace with and heal the traumas of your childhood. Dis-ease is avoidable.

The most important thing we learned in medical school was that everyone has a different body type with a unique emotional make-up, mental outlook and mental conditioning. It turns out that thoughts, whether expressed outwardly or silently within, are much more powerful than anyone ever knew. We were cautioned that in every experiment—both in the lab and in real life—the person doing the experiment affects the outcome with his or her energy, thoughts and expectations. As new doctors, we were surprised how much stressful lifestyles and jobs can create an increase in cellular acidity, which can easily be measured. Common bacteria (such as strep, staph and pseudomonas) and many viruses live in the body naturally, but multiply only when the acid-alkaline balance tips to an acidic state for a prolonged period. When their population reaches a certain level, the body enters a state of dis-ease. The miracle of the body is that it communicates to us when something is wrong with our lifestyle, through the proliferation of physical symptoms that never needed to occur in the first place.

To achieve total health, we learned to place our immediate attention on all things "alkaline." Alkalizing the pH of the physical body is facilitated by the ample intake of certain fruits and vegetables, hydration and reduced intake of sugar, caffeine and alcohol. Unfortunately, most people get carried away with what I call, "the fun foods." For the mind, we aim for an alpha-theta state, which can be measured on an EKG machine. This type of brain wave travels through the nervous system to create an alkaline state via the mind-body connection. The fact that meditation could demonstrably affect the body's pH balance was profound evidence of the mind-body connection.

In the last year of our doctorate program, we worked in the clinic treating patients full time. We continued to discover that chronic symptoms of any kind correlate with internalized stress, perhaps from a dramatic emotional event occurring at the same time. The term *stress* is synonymous with too much harmful energy that builds up in the mind-body and eventually causes a physical symptom. For example, divorce, career change, survival needs, a move in residence or an unhappy relationship are stressors that can neurologically intensify symptoms of dis-ease. At the same time, such symptoms are part of the miracle of the human body for their very presence. They redirect your thought process. You are then more likely to consider lifestyle changes to restore balance and harmony, which naturally support healing. There are few victims when it comes to dis-ease. Except for children, we are usually the ones to bring it on ourselves. Traumatic diseases that occur with children and result in an impairment or death are often soul driven, profoundly affecting all those around the child to discover a deeper meaning to life.

There is a beautiful energy exchange that occurs when two people come together with the focus and intention to feel better and heal. As a new doctor and budding healer, I found great satisfaction in teaching others about their body and offering insight to self-discovery. When I am treating a client or patient, my whole being opens in some way. I become euphoric with the giving and sharing. It's much more than an intellectual reward. My heart fills to become "a cup that runneth over," and my body becomes incredibly alive with energy. How wonderful. I never anticipated that I would get to feel so much love while being in service to others!

As I treated more and more patients, something changed within me. Increasingly, I experienced and felt many different qualities of light and energy flowing through my body, which I was unfamiliar with. I had been trained to observe and look beneath the surface to reveal and expose what is really at the core of the symptom. I immediately applied this skill to the special phenomenon that occurred only while I was doing healing work. I was aware of the energy centers deep in the body, called chakras, and of oriental medicine's meridian points, which can indicate an excess or deficiency of energy. I understood that balancing these energy flows could resolve physical symptoms and restore a sense of well-being, but I had seen this occur only through acupuncture and some of the neuro-emotional techniques.

Some people would become emotional and even cry during sessions, and then they would be thankful and grateful. They reported that old emotions would well up and then quickly leave—as if a burden had been lifted. Additionally, the physical problem that had brought them in for treatment was suddenly resolved. About 70% of my clients had a deep experience of intense relief and upliftment. However, this did not occur with everyone. The other 30% felt better, but their experience was more superficial, as if they had received all that they could for the time being. I observed that the 30% group was not as in-touch with themselves as those who felt the greater benefit. I was certainly curious about why that was the case.

Something phenomenal was happening, far beyond treatment protocols and techniques. Testimonies began to flood in from patients regarding their treatment experience, describing their encounter as a spiritual opening. Many claimed they'd been struggling their whole life with emotional wounds that were now simply gone! It was hard for me to take credit for something I knew nothing about. Sometimes I would feel my own emotional release during a session. Where was the energy coming from that flowed through me and into the patient? I had to find out. I knew I was sitting on a powder keg of my own emotions from childhood; how was it all connected? Discovering the mind-body connection was so exciting, but it seemed I had also uncovered a deeper level of myself and others—the mind-body-spiritual connection. It was all pointing to the dynamic flow of ENERGY that we are generating within us and the energy all around us.

Not everything is mental and emotional, however. We must take care of our physical body as well. During the first three and half years of the doctorate program, I self-applied every holistic and alternative technique we had learned. I wanted to feel firsthand, through direct experience, the positive claims of their merit. I exercised every day. However, I still had severe mood swings and blood sugar problems that seemed to be the result of suppressed resentment and depression. These feeling are usually lumped together with stress as the cause. But where was the inner stress coming from? The moods never lasted very long, yet they were so contrary to my usual patient and even-tempered demeanor that I was perplexed.

I began eating organic whole foods with no preservatives or pesticides. I even called the growers to verify the truth of their food labels and found that many producers were circumventing the organic food or "natural" labeling laws. Every six months, I would fast for two weeks with fresh lemon juice, water and honey, followed by a week of eating just vegetables. Becoming a vegetarian did not work for me as my body type craved animal protein. I applied my nutritional training by supplementing my diet with vitamins and minerals; I also regularly consumed fruit and vegetable juices.

My body felt so light, taking on an almost pure feeling. My energy and vitality went through the roof, and I slept like a baby. When I resumed consuming coffee, desserts, alcohol or too much protein of any kind, my body would be in near shock with discomfort. I could feel the energy of my whole body instantly change. Eventually, I learned how to balance the right amount of fun foods by feeling and listening to my body. Listening with your feeling self is the clearest way to meet your body's needs!

CHAPTER 8

THE LOSS OF LOVE

During the last year of the Southern California University program, students intern with patients in a variety of settings. We spent time in hospital ERs, homeless shelters and free health clinics so that we could obtain an overview of care and get exposure to unusual cases. It was an interesting time. I finished my requirements a little early and made plans to take a month off before my final semester.

My wife had hinted at the idea of us moving to British Columbia, where she had family and dual citizenship. She emphasized that it would be a good place to raise the children; we would be out of the polluted city and breathe fresh country air. "Us" and "we" I heard her say! I interpreted this idea of moving as our chance to be a happy family.

The idea of the kids growing up in Canada was very appealing. Lake Okanagan is the organic capital of Canada. Apple and peach orchards were plentiful and free-range animals roamed everywhere and chestnut, walnut and cherry trees grew in abundance. All this was nestled around a beautiful, 100-mile-long lake set in a dense pine forest and full of fresh trout that tasted like salmon. I thought I had died and gone to heaven. Well, the decision seemed easy; I said yes!

It was an emotionally driven decision, nevertheless. I was desperately still trying to keep family number two together. I should have never allowed my children to leave California, but I couldn't have known Dee was secretly planning to separate and divorce once we got there. We utilized my time off from school and moved to British Columbia. The plan was for me to temporarily return to California to complete my doctorate and then become a landed immigrant. As I was packing to head back to California to finish school, we got into a bad argument, and she said she wanted to separate. It had been coming for a while I suppose, but still I was stunned and in shock. The thought of being without my children really didn't sink in at first. I was so hurt I don't think I was even in my body. She had timed it perfectly! I had to leave to get back to school. I was so angry I could barley control myself! What Mrs. Villa/Tahar had said about my wife was finally sinking in, only now we were 1,500 miles away from my home turf in California. What had I done?

The next morning there was a deafening silence in the house as if something had gone terribly wrong. I said good-bye to the children. I was not ready to explain what had happened and the potential impact this would have on their lives. When I looked into the eyes of young Angelo and Mia, it was as if they somehow already knew! As I drove away, tears began to flow. For a hundred miles, I cried. What had I done? How did I get here?

I was sobbing uncontrollably with a sick feeling in my gut. Suddenly, the interior of the car filled up with white, pink and blue light, and I heard the words, "Stop, stop here! Stop here!" What? It was Archangel Gabriel—I recognized the feeling of love. He said it was time to meet with the Council. I pulled off the freeway to get my bearings. I had driven over the U.S. border and into the Wenatchee Forest in northern Washington. I needed a rest anyway; my eyes were swollen from so much crying. I pulled into a camping area and leaned my seat back for a rest. I hadn't slept very well the night before. I began to doze off, relaxing in a sort of lucid state.

The familiar vision of the Council began to emerge—all five of my former Native American selves sitting around a fire filled the car. The figures explained that my current life experience was part of the plan of my soul. "The pain and anguish over the loss of all you have loved in this life is part of your destiny. It is in this way you will come to know the divine unconditional love within you. Current circumstances are reflecting past lives held within your soul's causal body. You have lived many times in a position of great authority and responsibility for the people, the tribes and collective humanity. The fear of loss and the loss of love are things you have carried for over 2,000 years—since the time of Yeshua (Christ). It is time to heal these burdens. You chose this life to heal all, thereby showing others how to do the same. This is a special time in earth's history for many reasons. Humanity is being uplifted by an evolution of consciousness, resulting in a tremendous increase of inner illumination and a new, higher state of vibrational beingness."

"This Great Shift of collective humanity begins to alter the 'veils of forgetting,' by thinning the vibrational energy that makes up these veils. This thinning begins to open our soul memory of our divine origin and also where we are stuck in the pain of the past. Your time of remembering is at hand. You have now reached the peak emotional state of current life circumstances, where many layers of fear have been ignited or are at the surface, ready to heal. Fear from this life, contained in your 'story of early life,' reflects the fear you felt in past lives, of which there are many." I asked, "How many lives?" They answered, "More then you could imagine, but we will highlight the most severe.

There were many during ancient civilizations, the most prominent being three lifetimes in Egypt and once as a high priest in Atlantis and Lemuria. Most important was during your time with the Essenes at the time of Yeshua, where your family and the majority of your community were tortured and killed. You later had lives as an abbot of Glastonbury, a Cathar, a great Templar knight, a Roman captain at the time of Pathagoras, a Jaguar priest within two Mayan civilizations and Incas, both ancient and more recent. You also had many lives in Tibet and India as a monk and a guru as well as five Native American lives. Your most recent life was in World War II. Before you incarnated into this life, you chose to purify all soul memory in order to enter divine unconditional love. To achieve this, you must heal any part of you that is stuck in the past, throughout the time lines. The 'living radiance' of divine, unconditional love within you demands that you let go of all that is separate from Love!"

With each reference of history came a fleeting vignette of that time. As I viewed the passing scenes, I could sense a greater part of me still in pain. I also understood that I was holding vast knowledge within me. My mind wanted to ask, is this supposed to make me feel better? But as I was attempting to find the words, the love of Gabriel entered my body. I fell into a deep sleep; I must have, because when I looked at my watch, a few hours had gone by.

After I woke up, the Council reappeared and instructed me to attend a Native American gathering that was going on just up the road. I was to join this gathering and ask to attend the Inipi ceremony. I wondered what the heck an Inipi ceremony was. The entire Council answered, "You will see!"

The Inipi ceremony, as I later found out, is an intense purification and healing ritual preformed in a sweat lodge. The building of a sweat lodge begins by digging a three-foot hole, where several heated lava stones are placed. A round dome, large enough to accommodate six to twelve people, is constructed from willow branches carved into poles and covered with a thick layer of animal skins. An elder usually prays for guidance and conducts the hour-long ceremony, pouring water over the hot stones to create steam. Also, cedar branches, sage, sweet grass and other sacred herbs are laid upon the stones.

Up ahead, I saw a sign that read "Native American Pow Wow," so I pulled in. The first thing that struck me was the sound of drumming and Native American songs of prayer. I found out that the Inipi ceremony would be held outside the arena in about an hour.

When walking toward the direction of the drumming, I experienced a familiar sensation of "coming home." The arena was alive with vibration. There was a six foot drum in each corner of the arena manned by six Native Americans per drum, singing and drumming in prayer. They sang and sustained the thundering sound that permeated us like a continuous heartbeat. As they played, my whole body resounded. There were many dancers in full regalia moving around the circle. My body wanted to move. I had to dance! Out of respect, I made sure it was okay and then entered the movement.

I didn't have to think about it. My body was moving on its own; dancing in a sacred way as if the movement of my body was becoming some sort of living prayer. After about ten minutes, I was becoming one with the drumbeat and the earth. I was entering an altered state, basking in the sound, the smell of sage and the feeling that the whole earth enveloped me. The earth was truly alive—a sentient being with presence.

The Council members whispered, "Good. You're remembering at-onement." A rhythmic focus seemed to move me beyond time and space, even though I maintained the full faculty to move my body. I entered a feeling of deep peace. An elder passed by a few times, looking at me intently with a strange expression of recognition. Finally, he acknowledged me directly and commented that it was good for me to dance. Right about then, I heard the Council say, "It's time to go to the sweat lodge." The despair over my life and the fate of my children had completely left my mind, at least for the time being.

I approached the sweat lodge. A few people were gathered around, but there were no signs or instructions. I noticed a couple of people sitting with nothing on but towels; they seemed to be in a contemplative state. One elder approached and stared with wide-eyed amazement. He said he had seen me in a vision early that morning: "The ancient ones were praying over you." He claimed it was powerful medicine and couldn't hide his excitement.

"What does that mean," I asked? He began to shake his rattle and said that seven would attend the ceremony and I should give the fire keeper a hand. I saw a man carefully removing a pyramid of wood that had been heating the lava stones to a certain temperature. Together we gathered up some of the stones for the center pit in the lodge. We carefully put each stone into place. Someone suggested that I wear shorts or just a towel because it would get pretty hot in there and so I changed. Everything was ready! We entered the lodge, all seven of us. It certainly was very hot inside. Once we were seated, the elder prayed for guidance. While he spoke, he poured water over the stones, making it so hot you didn't want to move. It seemed that any motion would intensify the heat. The elder continued to pray and put cedar and sage over the steaming stones to aid in the purification rites.

Suddenly, the rattling stopped and the elder began to speak in English. He cried out that we were purifying the fear within us, that we should call forth the greatest fear held within so that it might heal. Fear separates us from the sacred within—our true life! Again, he began to rattle and sing prayers. A half hour passed. As he poured more water over the stones, my mind focused on only one thing—calling forth my fear and not moving. Even my breathing slowed. I went in and out of an altered state but remained alert to what might happen. All at once, the people around me disappeared, and the entire sweat lodge looked like the night sky with a million stars. Then, out of the blackness, my stepfather's face appeared. Clearly, he represented the fear within me. With his bold appearance, I also found my inner power. I felt fearless! I reached into his mouth, yanked out his heart and threw it into the abyss. My body and spirit instantly felt lighter, like a great burden or weight had been lifted from my shoulders.

The ceremony came to a close. All the previous guidance I had received about healing and lifting my energy to release past burdens really made sense now. I thought I had understood it. I did grasp the concept intellectually, but it was easy to deny my fears until I had the direct experience of what was inside.

There is a soul design that directs certain encounters and experiences; it can feel like a great force that is influencing events. This great energy force of the soul assists our free will to experience the greatest potential outcomes in the journey of life. The design is loosely configured around birthing within specific cultures and meeting many soul mates along the way. Each soul mate, for we have many, holds a teaching, a reflection or mirroring of what we can't see in ourselves. Some call this karma but I have learned it is what is held within the causal body. In the language of energy chakras this design or force emanates from the causal body, partially manifesting our reality. The causal body is located above the head between the 8th and 9th chakras. The potential of the causal body is to bring resolution to all existence within its many incarnations, that which is unresolved, namely the healing of separation and the return to love, at-onement. In my core belief of not being good enough there was also unworthiness and guilt. It seemed everything I loved, somehow by circumstance, went out of my life. My marriages and children were now separated from me by extraordinary circumstances. I began to feel the enormous weight of the loss of love. I felt there were so many layers of pain that to enter this heaviness was too much to bear.

CHAPTER 9

THE HEALER'S HEALER

The Council said that I must heal all buried burdens of fear, which were exacerbated by my "story of early life" and the loss I carried in soul memory. How was I going to do that? Michael had radiated the energy of love into my heart, igniting the presence of the divine within me. This initiated the beginning of my awakening and helped me reenter the energy of aliveness, thereby remembering who I am. At first, I was unable to connect to the love because there were many layers of emotional wounding that I had experienced growing up. But with Michael's guidance, I learned that each step on my path of healing resulted in profound self-discovery; my heart began to open, and I was transforming.

From what I could tell, my journey was about accessing more of the love within and around me, providing a sense of lightness that hadn't been there before. I noticed an increase in self-awareness and energy expansion, accompanied by improved intuition, soul memory retrieval and access to innate wisdom. The more love and interactive energy I felt, the more aware I became of who I was not! At the same time, I could observe that I still had unwanted identities that made up my adult personality—patterns of odd behavior, insecurities, severe mood swings and depression. I was often defensive, jealous, and needy in relationships and very guarded. I felt far from my genuine, authentic self and was living through many facades. They seemed to have a life of their own. I knew this because far too often, I would overreact to a person or situation. How was I to unravel these identities?

In school, I had learned that energy channels or meridians run along many of the same routes that comprise our body's nervous system. Deep within the meridians are the chakras. These are energy centers of light, templates if you will, that make up our emotional, mental, spiritual and physical bodies. When our meridians are in balance, we are symptom free. When they're not, we experience either an excess or deficiency of energy that causes states of mental, physical or emotional dis-ease. Diet and environment do of course influence our state of balance, but the surprise is that thoughts and emotions, both internalized and externalized, have the greatest effect on our energetic well-being.

Day-to-day thoughts and emotions are generated by hopes, preferences, desires and what is deep within. These inner states shape our perception of life—to everything. We literally see, hear and react to the world and each other according to our beliefs, which are formed in the "story of early life." If you have experienced rejection—or abandonment, fear, abuse, loss, lack—a belief about yourself begins to take shape, such as a feeling of not being good enough. When you are treated with conditional love, the authentic energy of you (your innocence) changes to fit and adapt to the treatment you are receiving from your caregivers. The creative, vulnerable and genuine self begins to disappear. In its place, a false or pseudo-self emerges and takes center stage. This false self is easily recognizable in an adult by the many unhealthy patterns of behavior and identities that reveal themselves in unwanted daily life situations and reactions.

We complain, "Why does this always happen to me? Why do I always react like this? I don't like that part of myself. I am always attracting this type of relationship!" These are just a few of the repeated thought patterns of the false self that dominate the adult mind. These identities become self-fulfilling because we are focused upon them—manifesting the same outcomes over and over again!

When critical expectations or inappropriate responsibilities are placed upon us as children, we alter our energy in the hope of being loved. If you grew up in a climate of fear, neglect, corporal punishment, physical abuse or sexual mistreatment, the threatening emotional and mental energy in your surroundings can dramatically change your auric field. Powerful numbing of the physical body begins as the wounds of shame are internalized. Guarding and highly developed survival adaptations reshape the emotional body to assume protective, yet manipulative, facades in an attempt to please and be safe! All these divisive layers eclipse the natural uniqueness of you. You stop seeing the part of yourself that wasn't seen, held or nurtured. You are left with foreign patterns stacked within your energy field, culminating in a veil that separates you from you! The result is nothing more than the heart-longing question, who am I?

Meeting Catherine

No matter how often I cleansed and purified my body, coffee crept back into my daily routine. I love coffee because it gives me a short buzz and a subsequent calming effect. I was perusing the metaphysical section of the local bookstore and noticed a beautiful blue book with a cover depicting hands glowing white with light. In fact, the title of the book was *Hands of Light* by Barbara Ann Brennan. I took a look and quickly determined that it was a sort of textbook about energy healing and emotional wounds of the inner child. Eureka! At last I could learn more about what was happening when I worked on clients and gain more insight about my own healing. It was still early Saturday morning, so I headed over to my favorite coffee house, ordered a triple latte and prepared to read this marvelous new book all day.

I was captivated by everything I read in *Hands of Light*. The book included some remarkable full-color illustrations of energy streaming out of a healer's hands. There were many testimonials of success. So much so that Brennan had founded and directed a four-year college devoted exclusively to the topic of energy healing. Her own story was truly amazing. She began her career as a NASA "storm chaser" and physicist and then worked for twenty years as a marriage and family counselor. She was assisted by spiritual guides and could clairvoyantly see healing energy, healing light and the contracted energy of emotional wounds in the body. There were so many miracle-healing stories coming out of her work that the

National Institutes of Health endowed her school with a one million dollar grant. I was so excited! I was about to burst and I was grinning from ear to ear. Finally, I thought to myself, I can find out where healing energy comes from.

At that moment, a beautiful woman walked up to me in the coffee house, said hello and remarked about Barbara's book. I swear this woman had a glow about her. How does that happen? I wondered. She said her name was Catherine and asked if she could join me. "Of course!" I said. "What do you know about *Hands of Light*?"

"I know a lot," she said with a flirtatious smile. She claimed to be a Barbara Brennan graduate and had a healing practice in town. Wow, I about died and went to heaven, but then I thought maybe she was pulling my leg. She assured me she wasn't kidding; she wouldn't joke about healing.

I told her that I was due to graduate from chiropractic school at the end of the year and many of the people I treated reported feeling energy and relief afterwards. I explained that I didn't know what I was doing to make this happen. She sensed a lot of light around me, which meant that my healing abilities were beginning to open. A similar thing had happened to her. Before the Brennan school, she had spent time with faith healers in the Philippines. The love and healing energy there was very strong. The faith healer she knew was devoted to the Christ healing energies of love. She spent a year observing and sometimes assisting him. While there, her heart began to open and she knew she was meant to become a healer. The clients she witnessed were having miraculous results, but most of the time they left without any knowledge of why they got sick to begin with. She wanted to know more, and that's when she discovered Barbara Brennan.

Catherine said that those who become healers usually have had the ability in a previous life and begin to show signs of healing and awakening in the present life. That made so much sense to me and so I immediately told her about my Council of Native American guides. Three of them were Native American Shamans, one was a medicine man and the other was a holy man. She was very excited for me as she too had guides who were healers and light beings. These guides and light beings assisted her in every healing she performed.

I asked her where the light and healing come from, but she was focused on my energy and didn't acknowledge the question. She said she'd felt my vibration right away; it was very familiar to her, perhaps from an Egyptian lifetime. She could see several overlays of Egyptian garb on me—like images superimposed over my physical presence, displaying for her how we knew each other. We were a high priest and priestess with many extraordinary abilities. Her open third eye enabled her to see these things. She explained that when you lift your emotional burdens, the seat of masks transmutes. You then have the ability to see and feel the living truth that is simply everywhere! There is so much beauty in the world around us. Everything is so ALIVE! With an open third eye, you not only see more but you feel more, too. You are no longer shut off from the real world.

Her words made me think immediately of what Michael had said about the energy of aliveness! I told her I would love to figure out the inner beliefs driving certain behaviors in my life. She offered to help me with that. It is part of the core work in Barbara Brennan's program. We exchanged names and phone numbers and planned to get together again. Then she confessed that it was not only my energy she'd noticed; she thought I was pretty cute, too.

Catherine and I started dating right away, and almost every night we talked about the energy, the light and the healings she had performed during the day. I had a million questions, and she loved my enthusiasm. I pressed her again about where the light comes from, and where healing energy comes from.

Everyone has a natural healing ability, according to Catherine. However, some healers incarnate for the purpose of uplifting humanity—primarily those who have previous knowledge of the sacred arts. Retrieving soul memory is a powerful path of self-discovery. The challenges come in remembering why the soul has come and revealing what is in one's causal body. The path of a healer is difficult—and not for everyone.

Catherine reminded me about what we were taught in physics classes: Everything in the world is energy. Even biology discusses the cellular energy that keeps our bodies alive. What is little talked about, however, is the powerful energy of our thoughts and emotions—or our spiritual body, which is very high-vibrating light.

It is possible to see emotional thought forms and the spiritual light body. They lie just beyond the vibration of our physical vision. Most people feel but do not see these, only because they believe they can't. Our spiritual body manifests infinite qualities, such as knowledge and wisdom, and its true language is of light. It is connected to our soul, to divine light! In addition to universal energy, which is all around us, some (but not all) healers can access this light by prayerful, sincere intention: "Whenever two or more are gathered for the highest good." The amount of energy a healer moves is related to how clear the healer is, how much emotional burden he or she has lifted and how pure the healer's vessel is. Those who rely on a specific technique, such as faith healing, often haven't fully learned how to receive. Moreover, any places within the healer that are separate from the self will slow the full measure of illumined love that is available to come through.

Our human nature is powerfully moving energy in many ways at every moment. Consider that we can procreate life, that we continuously use our creative imagination to direct energy for projects at work, for survival, and in reality, for everything we do. This all begins with a thought and an emotional desire; in time, the emotional thought/desire manifests in the physical. Change your thoughts, change your life.

Humanity's capacity for the energy of ALIVENESS, however, is thwarted by the emotional energy of self-judgment, resentment and criticism. We all observe the powerful, high-vibrational energies available when we are giving and receiving love. This love nurtures, uplifts, harmonizes and fulfills. We can decide to be in the energy of love anytime we want. Equally as powerful are negative thoughts, manipulative thinking and abusive treatment! Negativity or ill treatment is low-vibrating, dark energy. For example, thoughts of judgment internalized upon self or projected toward another are harmful physically, mentally and emotionally. Man's inhumanity to man, lack, disease, war and even worse all begin around the gossip table. The energy of inner beliefs drives unconscious behavior as well. When a person's auric field is free of the contracted energy of emotional burdens, it expands and connects to where love and innocence were lost. It then flows to the spiritual body and even to the soul level, giving one the feeling of being reborn.

I could see that my question did not have an easy answer. Catherine continued by stating that I had been a healer before and reassured me that awakening to my own soul's wisdom would be an amazing journey. This is probably why we met. There are no accidents. Our higher selves connected and arranged or nudged us to this location so we could connect. What's the higher self? It's another name for the spiritual body; it is where intuition comes from.

Night after night at the dinner table, Catherine would tell me about the healings of the day. She was very successful with many clients. I loved hearing every detail. She worked on many types of conditions: diabetes, colitis, pancreatitis, cancers and mental and emotional disorders. Clients would come in usually after hitting an emotional or physical low, she said. This is what it takes for most people to start paying attention to what is going on deep within them. Some anticipated their next level of spiritual illumination. Whatever the reason, a core emotional event or memory would reveal itself. The client re-experienced part of the past in order to let go, thereby relieving any physical symptoms. Everyone significantly improved or completely recovered, depending on the severity of the core wound.

During healing sessions, the healer-facilitator may also be seeing the original emotional event while guiding the client to the time associated with the characters involved. In this powerful work, the energy of the moment transmutes back into the light of who one truly is. I wondered if Catherine could see the past, the actual event. I learned that she does. Surrounded by the healing energy, she gently guides the person through the timelines—as he or she feels safe to do so. Wow! How is she seeing all that? I knew it was because of her open third eye and loving heart. But I still wondered what performs the actual healing.

Catherine explained that several components gel "when two or more are gathered" with the highest intention to heal. This process involves accessing three kinds of energy—universal, or the energy of pure consciousness, love and divine light. The final piece is directing the conscious awareness of the client inward to the level of the wound, where one makes a new choice whether or not to let go. The pure consciousness transmutes false identities that have been driving unwanted subconscious behavior, and the light transmutes the contracted energy of dis-ease that is causing physical symptoms.

Catherine described the etheric layers of the human auric energy field. As she did, I could also see the layers of whomever she was describing. Somehow, I had entered the soul memory of energy, as if it were a language. I could do this too! I was amazed that somehow I knew about this! Catherine said that I was remembering the sacred arts. But I wondered how I could be seeing if my third eye was not yet open. The full answer is very complex and dynamic. The short version, however, is that my soul memory flooded in and, as we talked, tracked the energy levels of the healing event. Amazing!

I asked if she could open my third eye. Yes, she could. But what would I do with it open, she asked. This is an important consideration about the right use of power. Catherine warned me that I would start to see more of the inner part of myself that had closed down so long ago. She advised that the path of power is not an easy one, yet she was certain it was right for me. I agreed and was flooded by the high energy accompanying every word she spoke.

She placed one hand in front of my forehead and the other behind. I felt an inner expansion in my head, front and back . . . then, all I could see was golden light! She said it was now fully open to the level my higher self would allow. First, I would feel the expansion, and in a day or two, it would contract or balance itself. Opening the third eye is part of accelerated spiritual growth and comes with great responsibility. It happens only when one is ready and is always monitored by the higher self.

Everything was calm for a moment, and then Isis, Catherine's cat, walked across the kitchen floor. I suddenly felt the cat's body and sensed a place on her flank that was itching. In that instant, she stopped and began to scratch. Wow! Did I just feel the itch on Isis before she scratched? How did that happen?

Catherine explained that the front side of the third eye is our ability to see beyond the physical into higher vibrational existence. The back is our ability to feel more deeply, beneath the surface of the physical senses. This is how I was able to feel the cat's itch. When both sides of the third eye chakra are wide open, we have the ability to feel right through someone, to sense everything about them even at a distance. This awareness is a heightened state of our natural empathic ability and opens according to the unlocking of the heart, which is guided by the soul's unique divine purpose. The human auric energy field exists on many dimensional levels up to a very high vibration. The spiritual body is higher than the physical, the soul level is even higher and who knows what else lies beyond in the universe as we traverse the continuum to All That Is. At each level is the truth of who we are—evidence of emotionally charged thoughts, unhappiness, joy, wounds and so on. The spiritual third eye is naturally open in children. But where the uniqueness of a child is not seen by their parents or caregivers, the child adapts by contracting their auric field and ultimately the abilities of the third eye are masked and shut down. With healing, practice and training, however, we can use the third eye to feel each higher level, especially when the intention is to let go and heal.

I wanted to experience a healing session with her. Catherine agreed but suggested I should first look up my profile in Barbara's book. The core wounds are the same for everyone, but the effect is different in each of us. In general, there are five physiological archetypes of behavioral out-picturing. That is to say, when children experience conditional love, in which they are not held, seen or allowed to express authentically, they form false identities and beliefs because they are altering who they are in order to be loved—even if their treatment is abusive. Determining which corresponding wound experience and personality trait fits helps to identify one's inner beliefs. It is very helpful to gain this knowledge to facilitate the healing process. However, most people wait until they hit bottom with an emotional crises or physical illness to seek help. I knew I hit bottom with my emotional breakdown.

I explained my experience with Michael and what he'd said about love being blocked by "layers and layers of unconscious patterns." Catherine said the behavioral facades were created out of fearful experiences, precipitating anger, rage, even terror—and deeper to this, a profound layer of sadness from the absence of nurturing. Since I didn't know my father, this equates to abandonment and rejection. She sensed that I had also experienced sexual abuse.

Well, that would explain a lot. Such a violation must have been from my first stepfather. For as long as I could remember, I had an odd, scary recurring dream. And when Catherine reminded me that my second stepfather was a rage-aholic, I knew my work was cut out for me. My enthusiasm began to wane with the realization that under my mellow, mild-mannered exterior was a chasm of anger. Feeling overwhelmed, raw and exposed, I knew everything she shared about me was right. I sensed my resistance rising; there must be another way. My God, I thought, this is going to completely unravel my personality—who I thought I was. No wonder I always seemed so far away from myself. Who was I underneath all this stuff, all these issues? But like Catherine had said, this was an accelerated path of self-discovery, and I was well on my way.

Yeah, no kidding! Most people are comfortable living in their denial. They ignore stuff and suppress their emotions, but they are unhappy and usually dysfunctional. Decades go by until they hit an emotional bottom or physical illness and then wonder where their pain is coming from. Okay, I had hit bottom. I was not waiting. I was ready to begin no matter how challenging the way. Besides, I was becoming a doctor and a healer, so I must do my best. I would be a hypocrite if I did not do my own inner work.

Discovering Inner Beliefs

Inner beliefs are personal patterns of energy that shape our lives. This energy is stored within our auric field as emotionally charged memories of mistreatment. These perceptions lead to what we believe about ourselves, driving not only wanted but also, undesirable behavior. We are finally set free by the healing, resolving and transmuting wound energy back into the light of who we truly are. Inner beliefs also shape the quality of every relationship and manifest our reality. We are literally living at the speed of emotionally driven thought.

It took awhile, but I was able to identify more of my beliefs. Given my family environment, I was not surprised by how many there were. It was like putting myself under a microscope to detect how beliefs really did affect my everyday life. I didn't necessarily like what I saw. Even so, I must admit that it felt good to take responsibility and become accountable. With this understanding, I could more easily make new choices.

My core belief was "I'm not good enough." I felt unworthy from a profound lack of nurturance. Remember, a child wants to know only one thing: How am I going to be loved here on earth? If a child grows up in fear or is witness to fear, the child will dramatically reshape his or her energy in order to feel safe. This results in an adult with an inability to trust, someone who is guarded, defensive or insecure. Any treatment without love is abuse—whether intended or by circumstance. If the environment is devoid of love (such as conditional love that is critical, manipulative and controlling), the pattern becomes one of never expecting pure love and, therefore, leads to sabotaging whatever love comes along in adult life.

When I reviewed my marriages, I found that I was uncomfortable in my own skin, not accepting that my wives would love me at all. I did not know how to let them in. Unaware, I was too guarded, allowing my core-wound ("You can't be loved") to be self-fulfilling. This dilemma propelled me into constantly trying to fix my partner, the same pattern I had with my mother. My self-examination next uncovered sabotaging feelings of lack, fear (especially of success) and shame (such as expressing needs in intimacy). Many such patterns can be self-corrected with a change in attitude and by interrupting your thought conversations as you become more aware of deep emotional wounds.

Finally, as Michael had predicted, I began unraveling my facades and understood my severe mood swings and unwanted behavior. I had so much pent up energy that on some days, I thought I would explode. It was time for my first healing with Catherine, but we had started dating, so she wisely declined. Because we had grown close, she knew her expectations would color the outcome. Needless to say I was disappointed, but she was right. She encouraged me to attend an upcoming workshop by an excellent healer named Dr. Roberts. At his school in Sedona, Arizona, he teaches the Awareness Release Technique, which is a spiritual and energetic approach to healing. The mere mention of Dr. Robert's name and his school induced a ripple of tingling energy up and down my spine. That was my confirmation, and Catherine agreed it was the next step for me. Meanwhile, I continued to learn much from her about the mechanisms of energy and consciousness.

The human energy field is dynamically alive. The aura radiates outward from the center of our beingness. What is radiating? Energy! The energy of everything that is within us—thoughts, emotions and beliefs—extends about 55 feet, as shown by

Kirlian photography. Kirlian photos show the energy of light around and through the body, clearly recording thoughts and feelings. I experimented with my own photos, noticing the change of colors according to the various feelings I was intending. This proved to me that we do affect our energy.

Most people have an innate sense for the qualities of energy that others may be holding—whether hate or love. I presume this is why Native American cultures are mindful of every thought, act and deed, saying these will affect the next seven generations. I became mindful about what I was thinking and set my intention on self-correcting as I went along. While difficult, this practical method helped me become interactive with myself while being self-observant. It also led to more accountability and self-responsibility. We know when someone is being judgmental or critical; you can feel the energy in their thought forms. I wondered what the energy of my own self-judgment was doing to me.

Most people love the feeling of being around a happy young child. Happy children radiate the divine energy of love, joy and innocence. They remind you of what you may have buried or lost so long ago. When you heal the majority of core wounds, you restore the energy of wholeness, or what has been lost. This reconnects you to the unique and overlapping mind-body-emotion-spirit energy fields of pure existence. When the heart reopens, you simply come back to where you started—the innocent energy and light radiance of the divine child within.

CHAPTER 10

THE SHAMAN

I was so looking forward to receiving a healing from Catherine. She is an amazing healer, and I felt completely comfortable around her. I asked again for a healing session with her, but she declined. Her training and integrity prevented her from being emotionally involved with clients. I hadn't forgotten about her recommendation to attend Dr. Roberts' workshop, but that was weeks away. What was I going to do in the meantime?

Catherine encouraged me to meditate on this question, reminding me that my Higher Self already knew the answer. She was right. Everything happens for a reason. Yet passion and impatience were overriding my intuition. I went to the beach, found a quite spot and let my inner self lead the way. That's not always easy to do when you think you're not getting what you want. I resolved to slow down and listen—slow my thoughts and emotions, just stop and feel my heart speak to me. I must admit that my overall passion was often at an amplified pitch, making it hard to calm down most of the time. Daily, I had to remind myself to balance!

It didn't take long, however. Next thing I knew, I could feel the altering of time and space around me, and then my Council of Guides appeared in a vision before me. "You're going on a journey!"

they said. Where? I wondered. "Journeying is the Shaman Way! You must overcome your fear and remember your true nature, which is fearless. In a fearless state of being, you can walk between the worlds. It is time to remember your healing abilities. More important, it is time to reconnect with the many worlds here on earth, the in-between, the layers of human consciousness that make up the timelines of human existence and the earth herself. The earth is a conscious, sentient being, just like you, only the size of a planet. Many ancient cultures knew about the four directions: above, below, within and all around. To connect heaven on earth, you must remember the kingdoms of earth and her four great temples: earth, air, light and water. You are preparing to merge heaven on earth."

My heart felt the gravity in the unfolding guidance of the Council. Each step I took with them laid the foundation for something huge that was coming just around the bend. "Where do I begin this journey?" I asked. They instructed me to go back to the Native American church and seek out a woman shaman there. I wondered how I'd find her. I didn't remember anyone like that. They said she would find me!

The following Sunday, I attended Little Crow's church. I asked if anyone knew of a female shaman. One person said there used to be an older woman around, but he didn't think she practiced anymore. After the pipe ceremony, I sat outside for a while. About ten minutes later, a woman of about 70 years with long gray hair walked up very slowly, as if she couldn't see very well. She inquired whether I had been looking for her. I asked if she was a shaman. She said yes, that her name was Sheila and she had arrived late simply because she didn't get around as fast as she used to. I asked how she knew I was looking for her. She claimed that the earth had spoken that morning saying someone needed her help. The earth said that he would have the powerful presence of Native American guides around him. These ancient ones had led her right to me. She explained that she was over 80% blind and relied on her open spiritual vision to "see." I asked if she would perform a healing session on me. She said yes, but not until the next week after returning from a retreat on soul retrieval at the Esalen Institute in Big Sur.

Big Sur is an ancient Native American site on the Central California Coast. Very sacred energy can be experienced there. Esalen is perched on a 500-foot-high bluff that rises above the Pacific Ocean. A natural mineral hot spring sits right on the edge of the land. She invited me to come along. Energy coursed through my body, confirming this was the right thing to do. The energy of my spiritual body seemed to be getting stronger, especially when it wanted to get my attention about something important.

The retreat commenced the next day. I agreed to drive her if she would tell me all about shamanic healing on the way. We needed to be there by noon. Since it was a five-hour drive, we agreed to leave at six in the morning. I was so exited to have this opportunity, and I wasn't disappointed. During the drive, Sheila began to teach me about soul retrieval.

When a person, especially a child, experiences a terrifying event, there is a risk that their consciousness will split. Part of them leaves in order to survive the event. They actually split-off or fracture from their soul energy or auric field. Depending on the intensity of the terror, they can fracture many times. There are a lot of people who are energetically split for this reason. This happens to nearly everyone who experiences violence. In my own practice, the majority of clients have experienced sexual abuse. The statistics for sexual abuse in our country is an alarming 65% of the population. I asked Sheila if these people were all energetically split. She said that many grow up in an environment of fear and will disassociate from themselves or leave their bodies, that is, some divide themselves. But they don't all split.

Sheila asked if I had ever felt very alone inside or as if I was not totally present, but far away. She wanted to know if I'd had life reactions that I couldn't seem to control. That's exactly how I had felt my whole life. I told her about my breakdown awhile back and how I'd realized that I had many false identities or facades to my personality. I'd come to know that this adult behavioral out-picturing was sourced in the many episodes in which I had dissociated to escape my stepfather's wrath.

Shamans heal by walking through the dimensions energetically and retrieving the parts that had been separated from the whole. The human auric field resides in multiple dimensions, each having a higher energy frequency than the next. For example, a person's intuition resides in the spiritual body, or fourth and fifth dimensions.

The physical body is in the third dimension. Feelings of overwhelming love originate in the fifth dimensional self, and so on. Soul retrieval is necessary when there is a severe fracture. Sometimes the split part is consumed by darkness and requires an exorcism. Soul retrieval requires absolute fearlessness and the ability to enter multiple dimensions or other realms. This is also known as "entering the mystical" and is always combined with love. In Native American tradition, if a child recounts snake dreams, it is considered a sign of great power. These children are groomed to be tribal healers, shamans or holy men. Many initiations await the child before he or she is ready, however. They must learn the ways of fourth dimensional earth and the elementals and transmute all fear that lies within.

Sheila suspected that I'd had snake dreams early in my life and perhaps was now having spontaneous mystical experiences. She was right. I confirmed this and asked what it all meant. She claimed that my soul was beginning to awaken and that knowledge of spiritual healing was part of this awakening. That is why three of the Native American guides on my Council are shamans. She sensed that I was here on earth for a great purpose. She had never seen anyone's aura filled with so many ancient ones, angels and divine guardians! A person who has snake medicine is one who can survive many snakebites or trials in life. He can shed many skins or emotional burdens of childhood and retain the ability to fully reconnect with the heart again. Healing inner fear unifies the whole and restores authentic power, which results in the ability to help others do the same. Sheila proclaimed this is what she saw in me!

We arrived at Esalen with only fifteen minutes to spare and entered the workshop meeting room. There were about forty or so in attendance. Sheila asked if I'd brought a drum. I hadn't, so she motioned for me to open her extra suitcase, where I would find an old friend of hers. It was the drum she had beat in sacred ceremony for over thirty years, and I was welcome to use it!

Sheila recognized many of the attendees. They were all honing their abilities to "journey," or enter altered states for the purpose of healing. It was her experience that one either has or doesn't have the ability to truly heal. For the most part, people who pursue New Age teachings are simply healing their own base chakras and restoring their soul memories about the ways of earth.

The retreat facilitator had us all sit in a circle and ground with the earth. We were instructed to lightly beat our drums and find a rhythm that we felt would connect to the rhythm of earth. He explained that each of us has a unique connection or energy signature with the earth and that we must learn to sense this for ourselves.

Even before the drumming began, I felt a great stirring of my energy, inside and out. The drumming reminded me of the Pow Wow and how dancing to the sounds of so many drums had caused me to shift into an altered state. The sound slowly got louder as everyone found a unique rhythm. As the volume escalated, it reached a unified cadence within an octave that flowed through my entire body. I expanded effortlessly into the drumbeat, into a state of at-onement. This place felt very safe, as though I were within the womb of the earth and completely protected. With my spiritual vision, I saw many corridors. It felt incredible, like being attuned with Mother Nature herself. The facilitator brought the first round of drumming slowly to a stop. My excitement was off the charts. It was all I could do to compose myself. "Wow," I mused. "I can do this; I can do this." The Council responded unanimously, "Yes! You are remembering."

The facilitator stared at me several times. I wondered why he was doing that. He described the next mode of journeying. To do soul retrieval, you must have many successful journeys under your belt. When a healer does the retrievals, he usually experiences a great measure of fear within the passing multidimensional auric fields of the client. If the healer is carrying fear, anger or terror within, he or she will not succeed in retrieving the soul of another.

We began again, but this time we were to set our intention and then journey with a particular purpose in mind. We were instructed to find and retrieve the parts of ourselves that had separated due to experiences of trauma and fear. The facilitator cautioned us not to be alarmed at what we might see because that puts the emotional body into fear and would reduce our success. He also reminded us that not everything we find was necessarily from this lifetime.

The drumming reached a unified pitch and again my body expanded beyond time and space, entering the multidimensional levels of my own auric field. There seemed to be many worlds with hallways and pathways that linked to vast planes of light and dark hiding places. These were all within me, as if I were as large as the universe. I remembered the Bible verse, "In my Father's house are many mansions." A strong inner directive guided me to enter certain areas, mostly the dark hiding places. There I found parts of me that were very scared and did not want to come out. When I discovered one, I found several more, and then too many to count. Oh, Lordy! I thought to myself. Why are they there?

It was at that moment I heard my son Michael's voice coming from the areas of light. He said, "During your breakdown, you remembered so many parts of yourself that felt far away, separated. You were experiencing the source of your invented identities and facades. These are the parts of you that separated to survive the violence. Emotionally, these are the parts that give you the feeling you are far from yourself. It is time to retrieve and unify you once again. These are memories of the past or burdens which create a heavy heart and push love away. Now you have the inner energetic view of your shaman self. Ask these emotional memories of the past if they're ready to come home, back into the heart, the whole of you."

"I will," I proclaimed! I could still hear and feel the soothing rhythm of the drums beating—the sound had united with my heartbeat, and I was still in an expanded state of at-onement. Again, I asked the scared parts that were hiding if they would come home with me, back into the heart. As I extended the invitation, this time with even more determination, a few rushed into my arms. It was electric. A lightness of being filled me as they reentered my core; but many others were not ready.

I thought I had done something wrong, and in that very second, Michael said, "Well done. The time is nearing for the rest to come, but not yet! To any heart opening there is a sequence within you, and certain outside events must take place."

The drumming slowed. I felt a vortex of powerful energies turn my consciousness to again gather and reunify within, and my eyes opened. Two hours had gone by, and we were now at the end of the workshop. The facilitator came over, leaned in so no one else could hear, and demanded to know who I was. Nervously, I responded that I didn't know what he meant. He said that my presence was energetically overwhelming for him. He had experienced such energy only a few other times in his extensive travel, once with a Peruvian shaman and the other with a Tibetan. I relayed that I was just beginning to awaken to my soul memories of being a healer and I simply didn't know much yet. He thanked me for attending the workshop because my being in at-onement is rare. It was uplifting everyone, he said. I thanked him for his insights and reunited with Sheila.

I shared my experience during the workshop with Sheila. She was not surprised. She said that I was on an accelerated opening unlike any she'd ever seen before. Since the next day's session would be only a half day, she encouraged me to skip it and enjoy the hot springs and get a massage. The massage tables were set up right on the edge of the bluff; you could hear the crashing waves right next to the baths. That did sound wonderful, and besides the facilitator had me feeling a little nervous.

The following morning, I entered the natural hot springs with time to soak before my scheduled massage. This place was magnificent with its sheer drop down to the Pacific Ocean. The day was sunny but cool—perfect conditions for the water. The body absorbs the minerals it needs right through the skin, rebalancing and harmonizing the entire body. I entered a deep calm—so calm that I slipped into a lucid, alpha state. And that's exactly when the Council appeared. "It's time to remember the elementals. They are spiritual, sentient beings who participate and interact with human thought manifestation." This made sense to me. I remembered that the physical body is 80% water, the rest consisting of minerals, oxygen and the elusive nature of light. "Yes," they said, excitedly. "The physical body is the end point of your soul's light; this light further connects, as a unified field, with the light of all souls."

The massage therapist came to greet me. I was so relaxed I could barley put one foot in front of the other to walk to a nearby table. By the time the massage was over, I thought I was in heaven. The therapist said I was the last session for the day. I was welcome to remain and rest, which was good news. I didn't think I could get up and go anywhere. Besides, I still had a couple of hours until I would meet up with Sheila.

As I lay there pondering what the Council had said about the four temples of earth, I began to feel very strange. I still had a body, but I was entering a greater, formless part of me. It seemed to be simply the consciousness of my presence, or "I Am," a pure state of existence. I didn't stop to think how this was happening. It just felt so natural. My awareness began to flow through thresholds of the spiritual essence of each of the four elementals, until my consciousness merged with water. As this occurred, I realized that I already existed in another star system as water, as if it were a simultaneous existence. When I felt the truth of that, with dramatic momentum I entered all water on earth. I became water for what seemed like an eternity! The waters of Life! I felt the existence of water in every form—whether as evaporation, or cloud formations ignited by thunder. I followed its return to larger bodies of water— oceans, lakes, pools, waterfalls—after which it reentered the soil. There, it participated in the creation of life, only to be cycled through to begin again. Water is never destroyed; it is simply ongoing.

I then heard Archangel Gabriel speak. He was explaining the nature of the great presence that works with creation to preserve the constancy of water. "You know this force as the great *Elohim*, a Hebrew word meaning 'God.' It is used 2,500 times in the Old Testament and is a uniplural noun referring to the Twin Flames of the Godhead." The experience of my moments with water was out there as well as in there and everywhere—an elemental at-onement. I seemed to slowly materialize back into my physical body, after which I sat up and enjoyed the sounds of the waves. I knew I would never forget the aliveness of WATER!

Eventually, I had to leave this most sensuous experience within Nature. When I met again with Sheila, she asked about my massage and claimed that I looked different. I promised to tell her all about it during our drive home. We packed up, said good-bye to new and old friends and drove off. I began to tell her about my experience of becoming water. She muttered something about a day in the life of a mystic and then began to snore. Sure enough, she was asleep. When we arrived back in Newport Beach five hours later, she finally awoke. She thanked me for driving and wisely noted that at her age, a good nap is invigorating. She offered to give me the healing session I had been waiting for. I was tired, but I knew she was going to be tied up all week, so I had better seize the moment!

Sheila invited me into her home and pointed to the healing table. Wow, I thought. No ceremony, no drumming—just like that? She instructed me to lie down on my back and said she'd be right with me. It wasn't long before I heard the shaking of a rattle and the sweet smell of burning sage. This wouldn't take long, she said, because it was not an actual healing. However, it would be a major step along the way. Awakening happens in a sequence.

She cautioned me, nevertheless. If she were to bring up what wanted to arise from within, my life would change forever! That sounded so ominous. But there had been such a long build-up toward this event that it felt like I had to go for it. She put her hand over my solar plexus and, in a couple of minutes, my entire abdomen expanded like a balloon to near bursting with heavy fullness. As I lay there in full distention, up came enormous volumes of anger, fear, terror and rage. It was my life in review. I saw hundreds of vignettes from childhood—the gamut of both tender emotional experiences and physical pains. I felt profound and utter aloneness and sadness. Every memory was alive within me, existing as energy within each remembrance. The emotional body stores everything that occurs in life. We carry it into every part of our existence. I could feel how these memories were responsible for each bizarre mood swing that had happened and for my blood sugar jetting all over the place.

Sheila announced in a very matter of fact manner that our session was complete. I was stunned. I thought she was going to heal it. She again mentioned that there was a divine sequence to my awakening. It was now up to my awareness to decide, to make a choice. She was quite blunt. It was time for me to go, she said before thanking me again for driving her to Big Sur. I was beside myself. What was I to do with all this?

Remembering soul memories begins first with glimpses of previous incarnations. In my case, all five of the Council—a medicine man, a holy man, and three shamans— were in service to their community by knowing how to enter at-onement with Great Spirit and the sacred earth elemental energies, the many faces of God available to us. What followed next would be like accessing a library of wisdom, an inner knowing of the sacred arts. The drumming was a simple way of using sound and focus to expand my consciousness to the greater part of me; it felt so natural. What had been extraordinary was my direct merging experience with the spiritual essence of water; however, we all have the ability to merge with the elemental essences within nature. As a result, deep healing can occur within the physical body because it is made of elementals, such as the minerals in water and in the earth herself. This is why the Native Americans refer to the earth as our mother.

My most profound personal experience while journeying through my own multidimensionality and at-onement was finding the multiple places where I was separate from myself, where I had escaped deep within, to survive terrorizing and fearful moments as a child. From this discovery, I strengthened my resolve to continue my healing.

CHAPTER 11

THE MOMENT OF CHOICE

I left Sheila's house staggered by the tremendous amount of fear, terror and rage I had seen inside my being. How could I not have known all these years about this mountain of raging energy? I figured everyone at one time or another goes through tough times, but I never realized how powerful emotional memories are and the capacity we have to suppress them. More so, how these hidden memories shape our personality and behavior in day-to-day life. In school I learned much about the psychosomatic or mind-body relationship and how our mind affects our physical body. From Catherine and Sheila, I learned the direct spiritual relationship of emotional energy and the cause of dis-ease, strange behaviors, moods and mental disorders.

Arriving home exhausted, I lay down for a good rest. The heaviness of the profound experience felt heavy and the feeling wasn't going away. How often does a person's whole life rise up within them like that? I quickly fell asleep. I awakened suddenly to a more lucid state and felt the familiar presence of Archangel Gabriel. I listened within for his wisdom.

It is almost time for your heart to open. You incarnated with specific experiences arranged by design. You, we, all of us, knew that for you to convey the Message to mankind, you would have to experience all seven core wounds of humanity and all the behavioral out-picturing of these emotional wounds. We agreed before you were born that this was the best way to receive divine, unconditional love, and then become a messenger of God conveying to others the language of today's human condition.

The human energy field has a tremendous capacity to love, perform miracles, heal and indeed move mountains. It has an equal tremendous capacity to experience pain and suffering. It is the core wounds of humanity within your soul design, in each incarnation, that lead the way to self- discovery, thereby opening the heart, transmuting trauma and creating an even greater capacity to love. Unfortunately, earth beings at this time are subject to a crescendo of fear—the energetic projection of man's inhumanity to man. All messengers must live through and recognize the pain of collective humanity in order to be the message of the living truth—"The truth shall set you free."

As quickly as Gabriel had come, he left. I slept for hours. Dazed from so much occurring in such a short time, I noticed that I had a few phone messages. Catherine wanted to meet for coffee in the morning, and my daughter Mia was about to have a birthday in Canada. Mia wanted to know if I would come up to see her.

116

I met with Catherine the following morning. I couldn't wait to tell her what had happened at Esalen. I shared my experience of profound peace in the moment of at-onement and how it all felt so natural. Her eyes widened as I explained details of the "journeying" and of merging with the Elohim and Elementals of water. Tears came to her eyes as she expressed happiness for me. She said it is a rare gift to be able to travel in and out of at-onement.

She reminded me about Dr. Roberts' upcoming appearance. He was scheduled to do a three-day event in Anaheim in ten days. As she handed me his promotional flyer, light and energy coursed through my whole body. I knew by then that when my feeling-body is infused with light, truth is being spoken. Attending this healing event would certainly be in my highest good. Catherine informed me that she was leaving town to visit a "Christed" healer, someone she had studied with in the Philippines. Christed healers work by holding the Bible in one hand and placing the other hand over the client. They embrace a profound focus of trust, faith and hope for whomever is before them—and miracles happen. Her adventure sounded exciting. I was delighted for her, but a little sad that she was going away.

The next day, I flew to Canada to visit my children. I had to pack and depart quickly to be on time for Mia's seventh birthday. Tears came to my eyes at the thought of reuniting with my babies. My life seemed to be moving at the speed of light these days. I decided to stay at a motel. The separation and pending divorce from their mother, Dee, was still fresh in my mind.

Upon arriving, I instantly noticed the tremendous life force in the air and how beautiful Canada is. The children live in a small town on Lake Okanagan, where the air and water are so fresh. I drove over to help prepare for the celebration, and Dee greeted me at the door. The tension, still between us, was hard to ignore but we pretended to be cordial for the sake of the children. However, within an hour, Dee disclosed new information about the divorce that enraged me. She had managed to finalize the details in my absence and now had sole legal custody of the children! When I asked how that was possible, she explained that her official reason for the divorce was that I had been absent for a long time. Never mind that we both knew the plan was for me to finish school and then move to Canada!

The emptiness and emotional pain of not being with my children was heart crushing. I felt overwhelmed, almost ready to burst. We spoke a few more words, and I yelled at her. I had never been a physically abusive person, but the frequency of my raised voice along with my bizarre mood swings throughout our marriage had taken its toll. We finished our discussion and decided not to say anything further. But I was fuming. I went outside to the picnic table where Mia was sitting. She had a sad look on her face and was trembling. I asked what was bothering her and realized how deeply affected she was becoming by having heard her parents arguing so much over the past few years.

Some children are hypersensitive and feel everything happening in the world around them. Children watch the way we live our lives and they are imprinted with this behavior, wrong or right. In essence, we recreate ourselves within them—"The children inherit the sins of the father." We teach by example through everything we do or say, and through our actions and inactions. I felt devastated that I had caused her discomfort. When I looked into her eyes, I found much more than sadness. She was afraid of me. My heart just sank. It was now undeniable that the totality of the fear, anger and terror inside of me was being passed along every time I raised my voice. I now knew that my whole life had been in preparation for this moment—to make a decision either to stay the way I was or do something about it. I had to make a choice. It must stop here.

The rest of the children arrived for the birthday party. The celebration began, but my impact on Mia had diminished the possibility of her joy on this happy occasion. I remained quiet and introspective for the rest of my visit. During those few days, I brought my attention to my children's body language and the looks in their eyes. I could see that they had grown distant, not out of a loss of love but from their fear of me.

During my flight home, all I could think was, it stops here! The decision point that Sheila the shaman had brought to my awareness was clear. I'd made the choice, and I couldn't wait to attend the Roberts' healing event in Sedona. He is a medical doctor who abruptly started to go blind for no apparent reason. As his story goes, the thought of losing his vision led him to an inner choice that eventually brought all his focus to bear. He did intensive research on how emotional and psychological issues alter the human energy field and cause disease. He eventually determined his current ailment had to do with the loss of sight in a past life. According to his soul, it was time for that past life to be healed. This healing not only cured his blindness but also spontaneously opened his "spiritual vision" or third eye. The accompanying healing ability that sprang forth lies dormant within all of humanity.

My First Healing Experience

The day finally arrived for the much-anticipated healing workshop. As I walked into the room, I felt very nervous. I had no idea what to expect. There were about twenty people seated in the room, each one a little apprehensive and looking around for comfort and familiarity. It was a mixed group, but most participants appeared to be somewhat affluent and sharp, yet casually dressed. This helped my comfort level. I was extremely excited, but shy. I did not want to stand out, so I quickly grabbed a chair in the last row. I realized I was a bit afraid, even scared, and by sitting in the back row, I could observe the process of the others. Yes, I felt like a big chicken.

Dr. Roberts entered the room and sat in a chair in the front, but slightly off-center. It was a big, round comfortable chair, unlike the ones we were sitting in. I mused that maybe this was by design to keep us erect and at the edge of our receptivity. As he sat down, a dead calm filled the air. Everyone in the room exuded an aura of readiness, anticipation and fear of the unknown. It was an eerie moment, for each person was there to make a change in their life and they were about to reach a state of complete surrender. The mind stops trying to figure out how it will be done and begins "getting out of the way."

Dr. Roberts, a large solid man with a full beard, deep resonant voice and ready smile briefly told us about the healing of his progressive blindness and described what occurs in the healing events. After he finished his explanation, there were many questions. A gentleman asked why his chest and heart felt so heavy with pain. He had lost his wife in a car accident several years before, and his new wife was recently diagnosed with a terminal illness. Dr. Roberts invited him to the front of the room to stand facing those in attendance. With his spiritual vision, he observed and described for us the many layers of this man's emotional wounds. He detailed each chakra layer of trauma relating to this life, the man's two wives as well as past-life associations. Because this gentleman had come to heal, his prayerful intention allowed his suppressed pain to rise to the surface to be seen, felt and healed. We were told that the greatest healing factor—which makes everything happen—is a common prayerful intent to heal. As Dr. Roberts described the grief held by this man, a steady stream of tears and convulsing whimpers overcame him. After several minutes passed, he appeared to have transmuted the painful loss of his first wife and expressed a tremendous sense of relief.

Next, a woman asked about her relationship. She and her partner got along fine and everything was great between them, except when they were intimate. At those moments, she would feel an inner compulsion to immediately withdraw from him. She knew her partner's frustration was building, and she didn't want to lose him. This had been a reoccurring pattern in all her previous relationships. Dr. Roberts asked her to come up to the front. He looked at her energy and revealed the details of emotional burdens within her that were driving the patterns of dysfunctional relationships. She had experienced sexual abuse by her father, resulting in a profound sense of betrayal and distrust of male relationships. This had caused a deep confusion between sex and love. Her shame around this experience amplified her inhibitions, and her ensuing distrust created the withdrawal. As a result, she permanently maintained an inability to deeply connect with the ones she loved. The moment she heard this truth, she collapsed to her knees sobbing.

I realized I was witnessing healing in action and became keenly aware of the workshop's format. I thought to myself, I'm staying right here in the back row and the last thing I'll do is ask a question. I shuddered at the thought of being invited up to the front of the room, allowing such vulnerability in front of others. I just didn't think I could do that. The emotional dramas presented in each question reflected the uncontrollable behavior and manifested dysfunction in people's daily lives. It always related back to a core issue, an event or a memory from childhood. We heard about self-esteem issues related to early rejection. People shared their neediness and over-pleasing behaviors related to abandonment and rejection. And some had dis-function and attention deficit disorders due to being partially split-off as a result of childhood terror and violence.

I reflected on all my training as a young doctor, my experience with the Barbara Brennan healer and my own childhood traumas. I could see we all had one thing in common; our hearts were crying out for love. It was now the third and final day. I had been arriving early each day so I could snag the same chair on the end in the back row. I was still attempting to hide from the truth that was within me. On this day, I was late. I entered the room. Somebody else had taken my chair! Oh no! The only available chair was in the front row—right in front of Dr. Roberts.

Thankfully, a woman sitting next to me was bursting to get her question answered. Her hand was raised. I thought to myself, Whoosh. I dodged that bullet. Now if I can just get through the day without having to stand up in front of the room. She asked Dr. Roberts about the source of her chronic shoulder, head and neck pain. She'd had the pain for over ten years and had been to several doctors, yet no one could diagnose or bring relief to her discomfort. It disrupted every part of her life. He explained that in some cases of chronic pain, it is actually the spiritual body maintaining a memory that must be healed. When emotional pain is denied, numbed or suppressed, the spiritual body, or Higher Self, will get your attention by bringing up the energy that results in physical discomfort. This is to allow a new focus and intention—specifically, to uncover your denial that the emotional pain is there at all.

Before he could finish this description, the woman collapsed to the ground and began sobbing. Between her sobs, she described rivers of pain leaving her body. At that very moment, I felt a huge force come over me. It moved me right off the chair to an upright position. It was so magnetic, I couldn't resist it. I stood up, kneeled down and put my hands over her arms. I immediately chastised myself for being so presumptuous as to participate with her healing. I hadn't been invited, but it felt as if my connection to the woman and all others in attendance had suddenly become entwined by a powerful energy. Thankfully, after ten minutes, the woman seemed to be recovering.

I sank back into my chair, trying to go unnoticed, but of course it was too late. The woman returned to her seat, and again I felt a great force within me. With a nudge from Archangel Gabriel, the words just flew out of my mouth. I exclaimed to Dr. Roberts that I didn't understand why I had been so moved to assist in her healing. I described how when I had knelt down and touched the woman's arms, both of my forearms and shoulders went completely numb. He explained that the woman had been beaten repeatedly during an abusive childhood. My arms felt numb because my energy resonated with the wound energy coming off her arms and shoulders. The pose of raising her arms to block repeated hitting and whipping had found an energetic resonance within my arms, for I had experienced the same. He went on to explain that my empathy also added to my ability to actually feel her numbness. Immediately, I knew exactly what he was talking about! The first thing we do when somebody is about to hit or beat us is to hold up our arms to protect and block the blows.

Dr. Roberts invited me to the front of the room. My heart sank, but at the same time, with the help of Archangel Gabriel, my heart overcame my resistance. I stood up and faced the people in the room. The facilitator looked sharply at me and wanted to know if I was ready to release all the anger I held toward my mother. I knew his insight was true. He had seen my deep resentment from childhood and the enormous chip on my shoulder. I encouraged myself, murmuring, "Time to let it out Frank! Time to let it out!" I could feel emotion welling up, and I felt like I was going to explode. I still wanted to hold it in, hold it back.

Dr. Roberts instructed me to put a voice to it. I squeaked out a sound like a little child. The facilitator shouted, "Let it out!" The next thing I knew, I was roaring! I could feel the energy of tons of rage and anger flowing out of me. My voice kept roaring with a life of its own. Incredibly, this went on for at least twenty minutes. It seemed like an eternity. My transformation was moving so fast, I could no longer see the faces of those in the room. Exhausted, I finally fell to the ground. I lay there in a fetal position, feeling as if I had been transported in time and was four or five years old again. A woman from the back row moved to the front of the room to lie on the floor with me. She gently wrapped her body around mine. It felt as if Mother Mary herself were holding the Divine Child within me. I whimpered and cried like a baby. I had never experienced love like this in the arms of a woman. I was so grateful. Later, I learned that this woman had a unique healing gift; the ability to transform lost innocence through her whole body.

Dr. Roberts finished his last half hour of discourse while the healer still had her body wrapped around me on the floor. At last, the day concluded, we rose and I could not stop hugging the woman. I felt she had saved my life. I had such a profound feeling of gratitude that I did not want to leave the rapture of her embrace. In her humility, she withdrew, thanking me for the opportunity to help. For this kindness, she too had received a gift of the heart. I felt enormously lighter as if a huge weight had lifted. I was aware, however, that there was more. The presence of love was thick in the air; no one wanted to leave that day. Five or six of those in attendance slowly approached me one-by-one, wanting to embrace and thanking me for the upliftment they had also received. At each person's touch, I felt a huge golden light engulf us both. I realized that our hearts were merging in at-onement. In fact, there were two who were very special to me, Mary Lou and Jennifer. I saw their light, their beingness as part of my true family, a soul group within a soul group. I sobbed, for I didn't want to leave them. We all agreed to stay in touch and decided our first meeting would be to attend Dr. Roberts' upcoming healing intensive in Sedona. We were so excited!

During a healing event, the energy is electric because there are so many in the room who sincerely want to heal some part of their lives. This magical energy is coming from each person; our hearts are crying out to love some part of us again. A clairvoyant would view this phenomenon as the golden energy of each heart chakra unifying into the One Heart. The outcome is an accelerated healing potential that builds exponentially as the day passes! It feels like you are being held by every other heart in the room by virtue of everyone's sincere intention and commitment to change. When I stood in front of the room, I could feel the energy of everyone. The energy flowed right through my physical body and into the storehouse of my anger and rage. Then the facilitator guided me into my emotional body, stating that the contracted energy had begun with early memories of my mother not protecting me. When he said that, my whole body contracted with resistance. Then, I began to let go.

There was so much pain. I could feel one layer after another lift at the same time the energy of love was flowing through. I felt the profound grace of Mother Mary move through me while the woman was wrapped around me. Afterward, she stated that she had received a healing as well! Sheila was right. If I were to bring my wounded energy to the surface, my life would change forever. I never felt so light and alive. As my son Michael had said, it was time to lift the burdens on my heart and remember the energy of aliveness. At the end of the seminar, I was feeling so much love. Gabriel whispered, "This is a good beginning, yet there is more to come." I then heard him say, "The kingdom of heaven is within." If heaven is where freedom is, that's where I was going. I set a powerful intention to go deeper into the healing experience, as I prepare for the Sedona healing event I was scheduled to attend.

CHAPTER 12

SOULMERGING™

Entering the Light of Heaven

Preparing for Soulmerging

I had no idea of the extraordinary experience awaiting me. This would reveal the divine purpose of my life, a heart opening so big that it would change my course forever. I arrived at my next healing intensive, a five-day event in Sedona, Arizona. As I entered the building, my feeling body was electric with excitement; the hair on my arms was standing on end. I had felt the sensation of high energy flowing through me before. Whenever it did, either truth was being spoken or I was definitely heading in the right direction.

I observed the room and noted there were about 100 in attendance. I spoke to several people and discovered the group was a mix of budding healers, people who had prior healing experiences and some who had no healing experience at all. All walks of life were present. They all seemed to have varying degrees of intention. Some wanted to heal and transmute the burdens within, learn how to access their spiritual nature and even discover the light of their soul. Others wanted to access greater energy and healing abilities, which would require interaction with the higher self and the intention to expand into soul-level awareness. Everyone knew they would awaken in some way, enter more self-awareness and bring forth a change in their life for the better. The participants looked as if they had discovered something or knew a great secret. I noticed a quality of lightness about them; they were beaming with hope and positivity.

Dr. Roberts led the healing intensive with the assistance of six other clairvoyant healers. The healers each had unique gifts, giving them the ability to see into the body and the higher dimensions. At first, all in attendance participated in guided energy exercises and demonstrations that lasted for several hours each morning. We divided into groups of two and three and then came back into the group as a whole. By direct experience, we were shown how to see, feel, sense and intuit the continuum of energy from emotional wounding to heartfelt healing energy.

Each chakra of light has its own energy signature, which can be felt and seen. We were guided into the chakras and their unique templates of energy, which together make up the physical, emotional, mental and spiritual bodies. The golden light of the soul is the origin of the chakras, vibrating from the fifth through thirteenth dimensional levels. We are literally seven overlapping spheres of energy that emanate from our souls. Each sphere of light is vibrating at a different rate from the others, a variation that can be felt as its own signature.

The endpoints of our overlapping spheres of light are the four bodies of existence—physical, mental, emotional and spiritual.

Unfortunately, most people primarily live in their mind (the mental body)—the nonstop racing and churning of thoughts. Trapped within the mind, people seldom connect with their physical body, and rarely, if ever connect with their emotions (emotional body) and almost never access the spiritual body. The secret then is learning to feel your way, rather than think your way, through life. The journey further becomes learning how to navigate and interact with all four bodies of existence. When we unify our four bodies of existence, the path of self discovery accelerates.

Our emotional body holds all memories; whether loving, terrifying or fearful the memories are still alive as energy within us. Emotional memories of happiness, love and joy remain luminous within our auric field. That's why we light up when remembering or doing something that brings us joy. Emotional memories of hurt, pain or neglect are contracted pockets of energy known as burdens, which undermine our lives through the subconscious and unconscious mind. Wound energy darkens the auric field, so much so that it becomes unrecognizable. These dark energies make us feel sad, depressed, angry, less confident, etc. The greatest amount of internalized stress is sourced in painful emotional memories. These lay the energetic foundation for dis-ease.

We, for the most part, feel separate and even cut off from our spiritual source of inner truth, constantly longing to be whole, to love and be loved and be free of the burdens within. Meanwhile, everything we long for is within us, the last place we have thought to look. After learning to experience and become interactive with the inner energy, we can access each of the four bodies and begin to open the doors to healing and the mystical or expanded self. We enter the flow of universal energy that is all around us. It is from this holy alignment or whole state of being that we open the inner door to the Soulmerging transformation, thereby entering the "language of light." When "two or more are gathered in holy alignment" (the inner and outer union of love and light) with the sincere, prayerful intention to heal, the collective healing energy of the whole becomes exponentially accelerated. Core wounds transmute as our energy magnifies with heightened vibration, resulting in a new state of being that is permanent and life changing.

It was rumored that at each event a few students would enter the Soulmerging experience. What on earth did they mean by Soulmerging? Was this a healing technique? Could they possibly mean actually experiencing the soul somehow? Whatever the term meant, I was intrigued. At the end of the first day, the first two people were experiencing the Soulmerging. I could hear a few of the staff members talking about this. They would begin to see an individual's soul light descending from the higher dimensions into the crown chakra, reaching the divine soul spark at the center of each chakra. Like an energetic implosion, then explosion, divine light radiated out in large rings of loving energy throughout the room. It is unmistakable when someone enters Holy Communion because everyone feels such intense love. Oh, my God! Was this really possible? The look that came over their faces was luminous; I could see it with my physical eyes and feel love radiating. Oh my God, I said to myself! This is unbelievable! Memories of my experiences with Michael, Gabriel and the Council flashed by—every amazing moment seemed to lead to something greater.

A New Level of Being

After three days, my ability to focus and concentrate inward became much stronger. I didn't know what would happen, but I could feel I was going to get there, wherever there was. Using my will and desire to penetrate deep within, layer after layer, I intended to reach the core, the tender and vulnerable places hidden deep in subconscious and unconscious memory. Once I figured out that it was all about memory or the "memoric body," I let go and allowed the process to unfold. I passed through thresholds of resistance and numbness we call armor, which energetically protects us from the residue of wounding. I could feel every nuance along the way. As I traveled inward, layer by layer, occasionally I would pass through pockets of resistance requiring an inner surrender so that I could continue. As I relaxed into the memories, I was able to flow through them which then allowed me to go deeper and deeper within toward the core wounds of my humanity. I could see and feel moments of abuse I had forgotten. Memories, and the emotional pain attached to the memories were flooding my mind and body—I was a four-year-old boy shivering with terror. Maintaining ever-increasing vigilance, I would reach another and yet another painful vignette.

At the same time, my adult mind wanted to deny the horrible events had ever happened. How and why could people hurt each other in this way? Fear and terror rose up through my feeling body, while loving energy from somewhere deep within began filling the holes where the terrifying memories had been. I was literally transmuting the fear within me to the energy of love and light, layer after layer. I continued to use my breath and focus, sometimes dry heaving in a cathartic way as clouds of anger and rage departed. I was getting the sense that what was transmuting in my emotional body had come from more than just my childhood. I had lived before. Somehow, I was accessing a new level of being. It was the causal body of the soul, where I had tapped into unresolved soul memory that was not at peace. When this energy is not cleared during one's past lifetime, it automatically carries over into the next lifetime.

I had to keep going! A momentum or powerful inner will was taking on a life of its own. It drew me deeper and deeper. How could so much pain be inside of just one person? Our human capacity for pain or love is beyond mental description. My eyes were red from so much weeping. My egoic mind became overpowered by a new part of me that I was discovering. It was the divine will and divine mind within me that was now taking charge of this transformation. I felt this begin to override any thoughts of limit or doubt. "Thy will be done on earth as it is in heaven," I inwardly repeated. Hours of intense focus and desire summoned a much bigger and more powerful part of me as divine mind was taking over. It summoned soul light from the third chakra, magnifying divine will. This pure consciousness is one of the three faces of God, I later learned. I could feel an enormous inner strength building within and calling me to keep going.

I passed through what seemed like hell—scenes right out of *Dante's Inferno*. Still, I had to keep going, passing through multiple doors and dimensional thresholds, and finally ... I gasped! I could feel a fluttering sensation in my third chakra and then my heart. Deep within my chest, a place began to open, slowly at first and then rapidly. Light appeared in the center of my chakras. It sequenced a concert of illumination, especially in my heart and solar plexus. As the light grew brighter, this inner radiance began to connect to light above me. Massive rays of light descended out of thin air, linking to the beautiful golden and multicolored light that was present and growing within me. As the divine corridor of light opened above me, light poured through so intensely that I thought my skeletal structure was going to burst. My third-dimensional body simultaneously expanded into the energy vibration of the fourth through the thirteenth dimensions. I suddenly expanded into at-onement, entering the Light of All Souls, or what the Bible calls Heaven. Love and the golden light of all souls were everywhere!

For three hours, with eyes wide open and fully awake, wave after wave of love flowed through me. I fell to my knees sobbing with deep reverence and profound humility. I was receiving more love than my human self could ever dream possible. It was divine, unconditional bliss that profoundly embraced my ever-expanding state of being. In a deep state of whole, holographic at-onement, I was entering one union after another; my new self was at-one with all souls of our collective humanity. I realized I was in the presence of the source of all soul light. As I marveled in wonderment, I knew I was kneeling not before but within heaven, held in the hands of God.

I wondered if this could really be happening. As soon as I had the thought, a sudden flow of intense love arose deep from the center of my being, swirling all around me.

A clear voice said, "I am Archangel Gabriel. I am one with the center of your beingness, and I assure you it is real. You are being prepared to give divine testimony for collective humanity. The language of light must be experienced to be known; it accesses the mystical self, which opens the door to Heaven on Earth. You will bring the divine teachings regarding Soulmerging and The Momentum of Light. The secret teachings are held within you as the ancient language of light that was later misinterpreted. You wrote some of the teachings at the time of Yeshua. Many of these early gospels were found and later hidden within the archives of the Catholic Church. You are to partially ascend, from a third- to a fourth-dimensional being, realizing and actualizing the lost teachings of accessing the divine light within and the conscious evolution of humanity into the expanded heart awareness. Humanity is about to evolve into their next vibrational state of existence. This expanded awareness will become known as super consciousness. Knowledge about the nature of creation is flowing forth into you directly from God." While Gabriel was speaking, I could see and feel an intense golden stream of light entering my forehead with such force I thought it was going to knock me over. Knowledge and great wisdom was held within this golden light. Memories of the secret teachings and early gospels bathed my awareness. Accessing the Soulmerging was the beginning of remembering having lived before as the brother of Yeshua, James Ben Joseph. Gabriel continued, "The secret teachings can be retrieved by accessing fourth-dimensional libraries held at sacred sites in many different countries. Now that you have entered the majority of your light body, you will be able to detect them. We the Archangels, Mother Mary and Yeshua will guide you!"

Remembering the Sacred Teachings

Tears gushed forth as I began to remember who I had been and now why I was here and my divine purpose. In that instant, the feeling of peace and the stillness of divine grace calmed the intensity of my expansion, stabilizing the intense light still flooding my third eye. I looked up and beheld Mother Mary, radiant and indeed "full of Grace." Her presence began to soothe every part of my being, yet somehow I knew there was more.

She said, "It is time for you, my son, to awaken and bring forth the knowledge that is within you, knowledge so sacred it has been veiled within you. It has been lying dormant until now, waiting to emerge until the moment in time that would afford the greatest potential for collective humanity." Again she stated, as if she knew me, "It is time for you, beloved, to awaken." I had no idea that she was literally inferring that she had been my mother before, in a previous life. "It is my time to be with you and to restore the innocence and love that has been lost."

The overwhelming physical sensations of increasingly high energy and universal expansion continued to purify my energy field. I was taken through many dimensions, crossing event horizons and multiple poletic voids that were manifesting the consciousness of pure potential for creation. This aliveness is synonymous with love, which connects everything! I was entering the direct experience of cosmic consciousness in a state of maximum expansion, where I yielded my awareness to the "peace beyond understanding." This display of cosmic wonder seemed to go on forever.

Suddenly, I was jolted back into my body and felt overwhelming relief as burdens were transmuting before my eyes. Heavy loads of sadness and separation, betrayal, abandonment and self-judgment continued to lift. The feeling of lightness within increased to such a high degree that I felt I was turning into pure light. My life was flashing before my eyes, including every event that had occurred during the story of my early life. There were also memories of prior lifetimes, too many to count. Visually, it seemed unreal, but I could feel these previous lives, and the experiences were definitely mine. One soul memory in particular was profound. I had participated in some way before with the Soulmerging of collective humanity, and I was about to do it again. Humanity would achieve this spiritual shift by intentionally transmuting a unique proportion of its seven core emotional wounds, thereby naturally increasing vibrational energy into fourth- and fifth-dimensional awareness.

From within, it felt like God began to speak, saying, "Your willingness to interact with your inner self, combined with your passion and intense focus, has allowed this to happen. The source light of you and all ascended masters will be your guide; our universal knowledge is vast. Specific ascended masters will guide you each step of the way. For example, it was they who drew you to this gathering; within this gathering are many like you who are also descendents of the Essenes."

I looked around the room to see the hundred or so individuals still involved in their own transformation, healing one level after another. Awestruck, I realized my spiritual inner vision had opened permanently. Still feeling only love, I could see the golden light, the soul presence, of everyone in the room. The more I looked, the more I could see. I saw the higher selves, or light bodies, of each person. The light body is the spiritual self, an intermediary between our physical body and soul. I suddenly became aware of a heightened intuition, which I felt as an automatic-knowing ability. I could see and feel with great detail every chakra level of those present. More than that, I could see every place of contracted energy, or anti-light, which usually forms around a core wound. Each pocket of contracted energy simultaneously reflected why it was there and to whom it was related. It was just waiting for self-love and self-awareness so that past emotions could transmute back into light, ending the experience of pain and suffering.

Anti-light forms layer by layer with each emotional wound, each layer making it more difficult to access the mystical self. Gabriel began to explain from a higher level of understanding the sources of human despair and longing. This is due to misinformation and deliberate misinterpretation of the secret teachings, which further condition the mind into self-judgment and perpetuates the energy of anti-light. Man's "inhumanity to *man" and to himself have created anti-light, or energy that darkens the human energy field. Within your great book, the term **antichrist should be replaced with anti-light!** Each emotional wound has many levels to it, all connected to one of the seven core wounds that drive our subconscious and unconscious behavior.*

As my spiritual vision adjusted to their physical bodies, I could see and feel right through the four transparent, overlapping energy bodies of everyone in the room. This reminded me of Leonardo's Vitruvian Man, a two-dimensional image that expresses part of the secret teachings. Within each body, I could feel the inner love overshadowed by layers of contracted energy. This dark energy, called anti-light, was blocking each individual's direct connection to the unified field, which holds love and light all around us. The only thing limiting access to this high-vibrational energy was the contracted residue of emotional pain and suffering. I could even see and feel thoughts emanating from other people's minds. This empathic ability of the soul, explained as expanded heart consciousness, can see thought streams of energy with an emotional charge.

It is important to note that what I perceived at this point in my expansion was like watching a thousand movies at once while feeling, seeing and hearing every detail. Strangely, I was not overwhelmed by the intense information resulting from my experience. The Soulmerging process had now permanently taken me into my higher vibrational essence where I could perceive the living truth all around me. I was in the presence of pure love; without love being present, a person would go crazy receiving this volume of knowledge about humanity. My heart continued to open. Light was growing within me, above me and below me, infusing every cell of my body with the wisdom of the soul. Within this language of light was divine knowledge, which understands the infinite relationship among the varied forces of creation, energy and our humanity. This living truth is just waiting to be accessed by our awareness, a discovery that must be experienced and lived before it can be understood.

I was drawn to look above the soul light of everyone in the room, where I saw divine templates of golden light that connected to everything. In the space between the golden matrixes of the unified field, was the energy of pure consciousness. The energy of pure consciousness is the pure potential for all that is not yet created. It is highly magnetized and ready to manifest our thoughts, hopes, wishes and dreams. It is the source of our co-creative ability, of our oneness with universal consciousness. We are meant to enjoy the interactive wonderment of journeys and human experiences without end! At the speed of thought, we are creating vast worlds and realities yet to be fully known.

I was joined by archangels and ascended masters. They introduced themselves and all began speaking at once, like an orchestra with many instruments playing a great harmonic opus. This communication not only entered my egoic mind but also filled my emotional body, my heart and a new part of me, which I call divine mind. Multiple streams of light holding knowledge and the Light of Light in continuum, merged with my new awareness. It was simply a light that was emerging from within me, but it assembled as figures who introduced themselves as Archangel Michael, Ezekiel, Gabriel, Rafael, Ariel, Metatron and other ascended masters, such as St. Germaine, Kuthumi, Sonanda, the Councils of Twelve and of Twenty-Four, plus an ocean of light beings familiar to me beyond their mere names.

Archangel Gabrielle whispered into my ear, "You were one of the architects of the Lord's Prayer."

I thought, "What on earth do you mean?"

The masters' ability to read our thoughts is instantaneous, and they flashed back, "Accessing the Soulmerging is the beginning of remembering your life as James Ben Joseph, brother of Yeshua. You lived in a small community called the Essenes; those who lived from the golden essence within." A deep knowingness began to fill me.

"Universal energy is alive and all around us," Gabriel said. "The Lord's Prayer, in its original language of ancient Aramaic, gives access to Heaven on Earth while one is alive as it was intended to."

"You mean the words of only one prayer hold the secret to how anyone can experience Heaven on Earth?" I thought. I then learned that this prayer has multiple layers and, once applied, provides access to a new "Living Way" that opens the door to the mystical self and the freely flowing universal energy of "All There Is."

Just when I thought I had understood the sacred laws of the universe, I was humbled again. I realized, nevertheless, that my spiritual vision and new empathic abilities were here to stay. I wondered how my life would be now—to know, to see, to feel so much. Then I looked up as I felt the gentle calling from twelve seraphim angels hovering mid-air in a circle. Oh my God! More angels ... unbelievable! They seemed to be waiting there until they got my attention; then, each angel waved one arm, pointing to the center of the circle as if heralding someone of great importance. I was amazed by the special angelic presence of love, which grew stronger and stronger. Just when I began to question why, I knew something extraordinary was about to happen.

Suddenly, from the center of the group, Yeshua appeared in a brilliant white-gold light. I was nearly thirty feet away when I saw him. Our eyes met and, in that instant, he stood before me. First, the most beautiful blue-white Christ light poured out of his eyes into both my third eye and physical eyes. He said, "Do no harm," and anointed my beingness. Next, he touched my heart, knocking me to the ground with the power of his love. I could feel the gravity of the collective esteem held by the archangels and other ascended light beings in the room—Yeshua's love was Supreme.

With amazing gentleness, he said, "This is only the beginning." I was so overcome by his intense love that it took weeks to integrate the truth of his spoken and unspoken words. I could not fathom the future of worldwide spiritual transformation that was meant to unfold.

Archangel Gabrielle passed by my ear saying, "It has begun." What did he mean by that? "For the next twelve years, you will receive countless streams of light. You must follow the footsteps of Yeshua, James and the Essenes; then the time will come to fulfill your promise to God and deliver the living truth! You are the Messenger, one of the first to experience and then to remember the secret teachings of how to access the divine! Heaven on Earth has always been available to humanity, but there are those who have distorted the truth. Finally, you will be given the 'divine plan unfolding,' which God has decreed as the 'Momentum of Light,' also known as 'THE SECOND COMING.'"

The Energy of Aliveness

I finally discovered what my son Michael had meant so many years ago when he said, "It is time for you to remember and enter the energy of aliveness." A week had gone by since my experience with the Archangels, Mother Mary and Yeshua. What do you do after an experience like that? How would I be? During the experience, Archangel Gabriel said that what I had entered was the light of all souls, Heaven on Earth. He explained that the hearts of all humanity long to have the experience of reentering a place within that can be described only as love without end. I had been given a great gift.

I was still in Sedona, Arizona, spending a few days lying on the red rock near the stream below Cathedral Rock. It was easy to relive the light of all souls, which Gabriel had described as Heaven on Earth. Strangely, just by remembering, I was there. I recalled the energy expansion of my body during the healing event and the surprise of seeing the golden light of the souls of everyone present— but it was much more than that. The radiant light of those one hundred or so in the room had expanded to every soul on earth, as far as the eye could see. I had seen oceans of light beings; while love flowed through, I was glowing as a light among them all. There was an amazing sense of deep union, as if we belonged to each other as one great body of light. Yet we were simultaneously each distinctly present as a unique, individual consciousness.

Wow! Twenty minutes had just gone by, and my body was glowing! Had I reentered the light of all souls merely by bringing my focus there? I heard a chorus of encouragement from the archangels, declaring, "Yes! This is one of the many divine attributes that remains after Soulmerging."

You mean that I can flow in and out of Heaven at will? "Yes." This affirmation resounded throughout all angelic realms. "Part of the secret teaching is the ability to access Heaven on Earth."

I received many other divine gifts during my encounter that strangely had become a permanent part of my life. As I looked at the sunlit air, billions of tiny white sparkles gave the space around me the visual energy of aliveness. I waved my hand through the air and could feel these light particles swoon through my body as if it were water. This was not a spiritual vision that would come and go; the light particles were not going away. I brought my focus now to the red rock and the earth. A constant up-flowing of elemental energy saturated my physical body. The energy of the earth feels like being in the womb again; all around us is a fertile and nurturing quality that fills every cell in our body. This, too, was not a momentary mystical experience.

The earth itself is alive—an enormous sentient being, only the size of a planet and with qualities different from our human consciousness. Native American cultures and pagan worshipers called to Mother Earth, honoring her with sacred communion. I had no idea how literal the term *Mother* could be. I let my awareness penetrate deep within her, bringing my attention to the concepts of merging and communion. As I did this, she began to speak in a soft voice. "In addition to angelic guidance, you will also have my help.

Wherever you are, simply stop for a moment; I will assist you and point the way."

I contemplated the fact that the memories of fear and not feeling safe were all that had been limiting my perception and sensitivities. In this moment, however, I felt in communion with the juniper and pine trees. They were so alive, emanating beautiful red energy. I focused my gaze upon them and heard one tree in particular speaking for them all. It invited me to come closer and receive a gift. Explaining that knowledge of the earth's wisdom and history is vast, the tree offered to be at my disposal on behalf of the forest. The tree was helping me to understand. Every living thing on earth has some degree of consciousness, therefore allowing the possibility for communion.

You are able to access a heightened ability for communion, the ability to merge with the elemental forces of earth. This possibility is within all humanity. But the burdens that people carry are layered upon them, lowering their natural vibrational energy and limiting their at-onement with earth. The dominion of nature and creational forces, the energy within the essence of the elementals, leads to a rich and nurturing experience beyond the current belief of humanity. By accessing the god force within, the life force of everything around you comes alive.

No, I wasn't dreaming! A week had gone by and every day my experience with nature was delightfully the same. I had been living on the surface of life before Soulmerging. Now, I beheld beauty in all animated life, in the light that occurs at a higher vibration than our physical senses. I was wholly aligned with the templates of multicolored light that permeate everything and, in turn, are connected to the unified field.

The New Human

Soulmerging is the divine birthright of every human being on earth. It is a spiritual heart opening so big that your life changes forever. The following are some wondrous and lasting characteristics of this experience:

· A new capacity to love and feel loved that until now you thought to be impossible.

· A distinct feeling of the lifting and absence of inner burdens.

· The discovery of your purpose in life, your soul's uniqueness and the fulfillment of your heart.

· A new energy of aliveness and heightened sense of vitality (higher energy) that remains.

· A sense of profound innocence and wonderment for life accompanied by a new feeling   of freedom.

· The feeling of being continuously full of hope and positivity.

· A rise in natural self-healing abilities that were not there before.

· An increase in intuition and automatic knowingness that provide solutions…continuously.

· The experience of light within…. Yes, light!

· A "full" feeling that can be described as blessings; an energy that radiates permanently from your being and can be felt by others.

I went into the local health food store to get something to eat. This was my first shopping experience after attending the healing event and enjoying a few days of camping in nature. Wow! As soon as I took a few steps into the building, a kaleidoscope of energies from the people inside hit me. Because my focus was on eating, I began to tune into what my body registered as the best foods for that moment. I could already tell this was going to be an adventure, and I wanted to take my time. I decided to get a coffee and sit down for a bit.

As I stood in line to pay, I began to feel unique qualities about each of the four people who were also standing there. It was all I could do to keep a straight face. The young girl in front of me had so much joy; it was as if she were laughing on the inside. I started to laugh as well but quickly calmed down so that no one would notice. The two people behind me had beautiful glowing hearts, but they were feeling sadness as well. The pull of compassion was strong in me as I began to seek why they were so unhappy.

While this was happening, however, their darker energies began to impinge on my energy field. Suddenly, I realized that I was taking on their pain. This was not my job of course, but what could I do? The cashier had a smile on her face, but on the inside she was grieving the death of a loved one. Who she was on the inside was speaking so loudly that I cringed. In just the few short minutes I had been in that line, I was growing heavier and heavier, losing my sense of aliveness.

This can't be right, I thought. Archangel Gabriel whispered in my ear, "Seek the beauty of each soul, my son." I looked into their hearts, seeing the love and uniqueness within. I focused further and began to see the light of their souls. Like magic, I started to feel better. And, oddly, their auric fields began to partially illuminate which looked like sparklers from the fourth of July. Gabriel whispered, "When someone is truly seen as he or she is no prayerful words need to be uttered. The person has received a blessing simply because you have sought and seen the beauty within."

This is amazing, I thought to myself. I sat down to drink my coffee, still thinking about what I would eat. There were many people in the store, and it was not that easy to see everyone's beauty in every second. Each person seemed like such a combination of hope, positivity and sadness. In those simple moments of curiosity, however, mental thoughts pushed through my forehead into each person there in order to find out why. Gabriel said, lovingly, "It will take some time to be in the habit of thinking without curiosity. Inquiry must flow from the heart-mind, not the mind between your ears." He taught me that most of humanity lives from the mind, pushing along thoughts that formulate as streams of energy, all traveling toward their intended target of inquiry. This leaves the auric energy around you vulnerable to the impingement of heavy energy from others.

I walked past the aisle with organic foods, really wanting a bag of apples. As I began putting them into a bag, the chakras in my hand registered a feeling, a thought impression, that something was wrong. What was not quite right about these apples? I used my mind to discern the dilemma, but all I could confirm was that the apples looked wonderful. At the same time, my feeling body was signaling something different altogether. The produce man happened to come along, and I asked, "Where do these apples come from?" He looked at me as if he could tell I knew something and admitted, "Our usual supplier didn't come this week, so we went over to the grocery store to buy apples. It turns out that they were picked green and gas ripened with carbon monoxide. I've been on the phone all morning with customers who are complaining that the apples taste funny, and they want their money back. We're taking all the apples back to the store today." I began to realize that wherever I set my gaze, even on something as simple as buying an apple, a deeper truth would reveal itself. My awareness had expanded to a point that I could only describe as "super consciousness." Yet, it seemed to flow just like a natural ability.

After being in the store, I was overwhelmed to be feeling so much all the time. It was a lot to get used to. While driving down the road toward home, I saw that the car behind me was following a little too closely. I wouldn't have noticed, but I could feel an energy rushing right through the back of my body and forward to some destination other than my own. I pulled over to let the person pass. As the car drove by, I could see a body that wasn't present in any kind of alignment; the person was completely pushing out toward a destination instead of paying attention to the usual safety precautions. With this observation, I realized that I was able to see thought forms. They looked like tiny gray and black streams of energy, perhaps colored in this way because some type of stressful or negative emotional charge was animating the energy. I came to a stoplight and viewed the people crossing the street. They also were focused on thoughts that completely projected out of their minds. All except for one, that is. I saw a young girl who seemed very happy and had light streams coming out of her forehead. When I felt these waves of joy, it occurred to me that we have a great responsibility to be aware of what we are thinking and how we are feeling.

As I had that thought, Gabriel explained, "The divine gift you have been given is the access to Heaven on Earth, which is the birthright of every human being on the planet. But there is more. The uniqueness of your gift is the ability to feel the energy of aliveness in extraordinary detail. You were sent here to experience Heaven on Earth, how to access it and bring this message to the world."

Feeling some reluctance about this notion of being one of God's messengers, I thought to myself, "Well, we'll see about that."

Gabriel responded with deep gravity, "Yes we will!"

CHAPTER 13

THE HOLY GRAIL

When Yeshua appeared to me during my soulmerging experience he said, "This was just the beginning." He did not explain, however, what was about to occur over the next several years. Archangel Gabriel spoke about accessing fourth-dimensional libraries containing the secret teachings. These teachings told how you could activate the light body within and access heaven on earth while still in the physical body. Archangel Gabriel said, "For the next twelve years you will receive countless streams of divine light." He also said that I would be led by Yeshua, Mary, and many ascended masters of light (saints) to sacred places on earth. Gabriel stated that I would eventually be given the "Divine Plan" and "The Momentum of Light." How would this all unfold I thought? "Trust," Archangel Gabriel replied. Feeling overwhelmed but incredibly excited I could not wait to see what would happen next.

Soulmerging Events—"The Gathering"

I inquired about Dr. Robert's healing intensive schedule but I found there wasn't a seminar scheduled because Dr. Roberts would be on leave traveling to the Middle East for an extended period of time. His healing school was focused on enlightenment and the mastery of energy healing. I decided to contact a few of the current staff who had experienced Soulmerging to see if anyone would be leading the intensives during Dr. Robert's absence. Coincidentally, the head teacher was formulating a new program which focused solely on Soulmerging. She told me she needed one more staff member and that she was divinely guided to contact me for the position. She offered me the position and I accepted. Soulmerging events were then developed and we called them "The Gathering." The intensives were five days in length, there was no formal instruction manual, nor was the seminar tied to an organized ritual or religious dogma. All religious orientations were accepted. About two hundred people simply came together to connect with God and the soul light within. This was a new discovery that was exciting; the direct experience of connecting with the soul was powerful and unprecedented within spiritual enlightenment. We maintained a divine and holy inner alignment and a prayerful intention to heal in order to access divine states of enlightened consciousness. Those in attendance came from all over the United States and from about twenty different countries around the world. Attendance grew by word of mouth.

The first gathering was about to begin. I was nervous but I felt exhilarated to be sharing in the extraordinary experience. During the pre-seminar staff meeting, I asked the other staff members what I would do once we began? They responded by saying, "Facilitate by energetically holding the hearts of everyone in the room." Facilitating is holding someone in a place of unconditional love thereby allowing them to feel safe in revealing very deep, dark and tender wounds. This is a holy alignment and intention that purifies your physical body as a pure vessel for the light of the father, archangels and saints to flow through you and assisting the transformation of another. I and the rest of the staff adjourned from our morning meeting and entered the large ballroom where there were two hundred in attendance. When entering the room I immediately felt the intensity of energy that increased throughout the day. I sat down with the staff in front of the room and I began to feel into the hearts of all in attendance. As a facilitator, the expansion into the heart energy of a large group was far greater than my personal Soulmerging experience. This was a new quality of love that exponentially increased throughout the five days. I entered a state of at-onement; a union of pure energy of the "One Heart." I immediately felt the presence of the archangels. At various times during the event, the facilitators would be spontaneously moved to channel one of the archangels. As the channeling progressed, powerful waves of love from the archangel would flow forth through our bodies and into the group causing deeper and more powerful healings. As the energy of love, waves of light and angelic presence intensified, those who were ready began their soulmerging experience. I could always tell who was about to Soulmerge because I could clairvoyantly see the divine corridor open above their crown chakra. The divine corridor looks like a brilliant light, opening out of thin air, above the head. This golden light of the soul is actually a stream of light descending from heaven. It is the very light of the soul, of the initiate, that has now entered the moment of readiment to receive the greater love and light. The individual would usually be transmuting part of a core emotional wound which then paved the way of their readiness to receive the stream of soul love and light. Everyone in attendance was healing and transmuting emotional wounds. When a person opens through sincere and prayerful intention to heal, the very high vibrational energy of love and light can be accessed thereby transmuting the darker energies of wounds. The result is a permanent lightness of being, increasing your natural light radiance. The secret is in the group. The power resides in the magnitude of the many in holy alignment with the divine. I could see golden light strands emanate out of each heart in the room connecting to a center point just above the crowns of all in attendance. Unbeknown to each person, they were connecting their hearts to each other thereby paving the way to profound transformation. When one person would heal or transmute a portion of their wounds it affected the upliftment of everyone else in the room. It is said that you may enter the light of the father by entering the power of the two or more coming together; Jesus said, "For where two or three come together in my name, there am I with them." It was so electrifying and powerful to experience the moment by moment ever increasing momentum of love.

Throughout the days of the event, as a facilitator, I did not remain seated in front of the room. I walked about the room throughout the day and became attuned to the higher selves of those present. Over and over again, I would suddenly be drawn to stand next to and touch the shoulder of someone seated in the room. They were in a healing process at the point of my arrival. I felt angelic as I facilitated the flow of healing energy. During the many lunch and dinner breaks we shared the experiences of the day. Eventually, one by one, those who I had individually facilitated would come over to thank me and stated they felt the presence of Archangel Raphael and many other archangels, depending upon what they needed in the moment. For example, one person stated that as I came near she felt fatherly energy flow into her; she felt the lifting of a very old burden she had been carrying. She said she was very grateful because her father had died when she was three. The fatherly energy was not from me, I was acting as a pure vessel for the divine to come through. There were thousands of testimonials such as this one. There are many facets of healing energy and also many qualities to the energy of love held within rays of light that will flow through the facilitator depending upon what is needed. There was always the presence of the archangels and ascended masters that surrounded the entire gathering. In special moments this divine presence that surrounded the gathering would expand to what looked like oceans of angelic beings. Tears were continually streaming from my face to the point I began to carry Kleenex around with me on a shoulder strap. I always looked forward to the sharing of our experiences during meal times. There was a common quality among us. We were all extraordinarily sensitive from birth. We all felt as if we were different in some way throughout our lives and we all had some sort of traumatic life experience of abuse, terror, fear, abandonment, rejection, and aloneness. We each possessed an uncommon drive or spiritual knowledge, what I call "the God force" to seek our spiritual self and heal. They also possessed some unique quality around the virtues of faith, trust, hope, compassion and love.

Gabriel was now in constant dialogue with me. There was also intermittent dialoging with Archangels Michael, Raphael, Ariel, Ezekiel, Metatron, Serapis Bey, Sonanda, Ra, Yeshua, Mother Mary and many without names. I always recognized them by their love. There were also many Native American spirit beings and occasionally the spiritual essence of the earth herself.

Archangel Gabriel

When Archangel Gabriel appeared to me during my soulmerging, he announced that I would be in preparation for twelve years. Whenever I asked, "Preparation for what?" He was very vague in his answers. After many attempts to find out more detail it became clear I was on a need to know basis. He explained it had always been done this way. During the first intensive in which I was facilitating, he explained that he was my teacher, and he was in a vibrational state of at-onement with the center of my being. He stated that it was very rare for someone to have an archangel as a teacher. He began speaking to me almost on a continuous basis. His communication came in many ways: sometimes telepathic, sometimes clairaudient, and sometimes he would appear in form or simply as light. When it was time to travel somewhere his presence became very strong within me. It was a powerful, magnetic, telepathic and nudging with instructions; meet this person, talk with that person, read certain sections of books, even travel to sacred sites in other countries. What became a little annoying was his monitoring of my thoughts, but I came to profoundly understand the wisdom of his teaching. Sometimes as many as two hundred times a day he would physically touch my face, communicating, "Do you really want that thought on its way to manifestation?" I would stop what I was doing and preview my last forty thoughts or so, instantly discovering which thought or thoughts he was referring to. Oh no, I would say to myself, and I would erase the thought stream by intention and in that instant I would see it disintegrate.

Our thought streams emanate out of our third eye as tiny grey translucent streams of energy. If these thoughts are of judgment, whether to ourselves or to someone else, the grey streams turn to black and begin to darken the auric field of the recipient! Whenever I was generating thoughts of limit in some way or extending my awareness to the past or future, he would correct me stating, "The power of creating is in the now moment and not the past or future." He would also stimulate me physically if I was in danger in any way—a potential auto collision or even a traffic ticket or someone trying to manipulate me with manipulative energy. I did not realize it but his support was profound. It took a great amount of practice to undo the mental habits and conditioning of my mind. When he stimulated my inner nose, he was confirming that my knowing or thought was truth. When he stimulated my inner ear, it meant that I was hearing the truth. He was teaching me to honor myself, to know the power of being in the present and to be mindful of my thoughts; for we are manifesting our reality at the speed of emotional thought. Over time I became aware that this internal dialogue drove my outlook, behavior and daily life experiences. Archangel Gabriel stated, "All is given according to belief." Reoccurring thoughts become beliefs. Therefore, thoughts become self-fulfilling prophesy. I also discovered how my mind was packed with modern day advertising slogans, oral traditions, parental criticisms, etc. It was time to take out the trash piling up in my mind and so I began the new habit of self correcting my thoughts on an ongoing basis. After all, who is in charge? I am.

The Holy Grail and the Isle of Avalon

"The Gathering" or Soulmerging events occurred about every two months. In addition to the group events, I maintained a private healing practice. Each week I saw between thirty to forty people for private energy healing sessions. Clients came in with a variety of physical and emotional symptoms. Commonly individuals were suffering from chronic pain, emotional life dramas, sadness, depression and grief...the list is long. Whether they were adults or children, something had interrupted the quality of their life in which they could not find a solution. As a result of my first soulmerging experience, I was able to actualize and realize the light within me. In private session, I was able to look at my client and access their light which revealed the truth behind their condition. This is because all knowledge is held in light. Accessing their light was in essence accessing the knowledge of who they truly were. Fully opened third-eye vision, is an extraordinary divine gift, giving me the ability to hear and empath the source of my client's dysfunction and reveal it to them. During the first fifteen minutes of a session, I performed this reading for them simply by focusing on the beauty within them and myself. For the remainder of the hour, tears would flow as I opened myself to at-onement entering the golden light of the client and myself and we would be drenched in the healing energies of love and light. Simultaneously, I could observe the dark wound energies. As I did, I could observe these energies transmute back into the light energies within the client's auric field. They always reported relief and the feeling of lightness, even happiness and joy. Some simply walked away in a profound feeling of peace. The sessions were always life changing.

One morning I began my usual twenty minute meditation aligning with the love that loves, the light of light and pure consciousness (the trinity) and Gabriel whispered, "Prepare yourself. You'll be traveling soon." "When, where?" I asked. There was no answer. Sometimes his communication was non-stop. I could not turn it off. Other times, it was so brief it left me a little frustrated. However, over time I realized the briefer the message the greater the mystery that was about to unfold. I couldn't imagine going anywhere. The weekend was coming and I was looking forward to the rest. At the end of the day, a client came in for a session and brought me a book about the ancient Abbey/Monastery of Glastonbury, England, formally known as The Isle of Avalon. He told me the sight of this abbey was on holy ground (very high energy). This was the burial site of King Arthur and later the burial site of Mary. Energy rushed up and down my entire body, my heart felt very excited. What was so important about this I wondered? He told me that Joseph of Arimathea, who had placed Christ's (Yeshua's) body in the tomb, obtained a chalice or cup as a spiritual memento of his friend Yeshua. Later Joseph brought the chalice to The Isle of Avalon and buried it near the Chalice Well. It was near this sight that Saint Mary's Church was later built in approximately 100AD. Over the next 1,500 years, it became the greatest Monastery of Great Britain, second only to Westminster Abbey. In present day, it is called Glastonbury Abbey. Legend has it that Joseph of Arimathea had visited the Isle of Avalon many times. He was a tin trader with many ships trading this precious metal throughout the Mediterranean. During one visit he was accompanied by the boy Yeshua, James, Mother Mary and others. When my client spoke of this last account in the book, my inner light illuminated so intensely I thought I was going to jump out of my skin. I was so amplified that I was losing my composure in front of my client. Fortunately my client was also a friend so I was able to confide what was occurring within me. I told him that I felt like I was being magnetically called and pulled to go there NOW! I woke up the next morning and the powerful force of the energy to go was stronger than ever. The moment I booked the ticket this magnetic feeling began to relax.

163

Within forty-eight hours I had landed at the Heathrow airport in London, England.

The Glastonbury area was a focus of some of the oldest mythology of Great Britain. The oldest being King Arthur, the legendary Celtic warlord king, Guinevere and The Knights of the Round Table, the quest for the holy grail, the ancient mystery schools of the Celtic (pagan) shamans and the many magical tales of Merlin. Two thousand years ago the sea washed right to the shores of Glastonbury and the bottom of the great Tor Hill, The Isle of Avalon. This isle of glass (crystal) is a center for earth ley-lines, or roots of spiritual energy which are said to link to all other sacred or religious sites around the planet. Near Tor Hill is the ancient Chalice Well Inn and Chalice Well. This ancient spring has three individual well-heads and legend has it they possess healing waters.

This great church, which grew over centuries to finally become known as the Abbey of Glastonbury, has been visited by millions. For fifteen hundred years, from within the initial church called Saint Mary's, the secrets of the Holy Grail were passed from abbot to abbot. Somehow, they knew how to access divine light and over hundreds of years the word of this special experience and knowledge spread throughout Europe. The passing of the knowledge of the rituals and secrets ended when King Henry VIII tortured and hung Abbot Whiting and destroyed the very structure of the Abbey of Glastonbury. This abbey now lies in ruins but is still considered holy ground. The abbey is a living Christian sanctuary in which there is an annual pilgrimage that includes the Roman Catholic Church, performing a mass at the base of the great Tor Hill.

I landed at Heathrow airport, rented a car and headed to Glastonbury. On the way, just outside Salisbury, was Stonehenge which held mysteries predating Merlin and the Arthurian legends. England is dotted with sacred sites wherever the energy ley-lines, called Mary and Michael lines, intersect. The movie, The Da Vinci Code, referred to these energy lines as "rose lines." At the point of intersection there will usually be an ancient holy site, monastery, church or prehistoric monolithic monument. For the intuitive eye, you will be able to see these magical energy doorways or star gates that allow you to travel energetically through the dimensions. Mystery schools were created at the sites to teach the initiate how to access the light of the soul. The light of the soul expands from the third through the thirteenth dimensions. The sacred sites of ancient mystery schools are located where these lines intersect all over the world, not just in England. This is the reason why the Abbey of Glastonbury gained such popularity throughout Europe—it is the former site of a Celtic mystery school. The energy is high and so people are naturally drawn there.

I sat within the circle of Stonehenge and began to see that the circle was indeed a dimensional energy doorway; more than that, it was a star-gate that flowed through the sun and into other star systems. I couldn't spend any more time there because the magnetic energy of Glastonbury and Archangel Gabriel were becoming very strong again, pulling me out of the star-gate. I arrived in Glastonbury and checked into The Chalice Well Inn, just a few blocks from the abbey ruins. The innkeeper asked what brought me to Glastonbury and I told her that I had been divinely guided to come there after reading about the abbey and Joseph of Arimathea. The only thing I knew was that my trip had something to do with Joseph of Arimathea and his story of bringing a chalice or cup as a memento from his time with Yeshua. Her eyes lit up and she said she was feeling very strong energy moving up and down her body. She said, "Come with me upstairs. We have a meditation room that is an exact replica of the Last Supper complete with an eighteen foot table, twelve chairs and a wood-beam ceiling." I entered the room and asked if I could meditate for a while. She said, "Of course. I will see that you are not disturbed. But first I have something that you might like to hold while you are meditating." She left the room and after about ten minutes she returned with a magnificent ancient blue sapphire encrusted chalice. The entire exterior and interior sides were embedded with hundreds of blue sapphires. I was stunned. I had never seen anything so beautiful in my life. Could this be the chalice from Joseph of Arimathea? She explained that she and her husband were guided here many years ago and never left. One day while gardening they found the cup buried in the garden. She said she slept with it every night because it helped her feel closer to God. She asked me to return the cup to her when I was done meditating. She said she would be downstairs at the front desk. Then she left the room.

I began meditating, holding the beautiful blue-sapphire chalice. Within a few minutes, a large six foot wooden Cross appeared and hovered above the opposite end of the table. I felt the presence of Yeshua and his love for me filled my beingness. As I gazed at the enormous Cross, I noticed that the four ends were not squared but had a three-point clover-like appearance. Yeshua seemed to be directing my attention to each end-point of the Cross as if they were representing something significant. One by one all four ends of the Cross turned into the brightest white light I have ever seen. When all four points were illuminated, the center of the Cross, which represented the heart, lit up large enough to engulf all four points. When this occurred the entire room filled with light and then Yeshua appeared and pointed to the Cross and began to speak.

He said, "My dear brother, have you not forgotten the true meaning of the Cross? Each point represents one of the four bodies of man. The four bodies are of mind, emotion, physical and spiritual. When unified as one from the love of heart the four bodies illuminate becoming 'the holy temple,' the chalice, the receptacle of the divine. The human body is either the Cross of suffering or the Cross of love and illumination. When light is activated within the human vessel in this way it becomes the receiving chalice of the divine, becoming 'The Holy Grail' which is what you are now calling Soulmerging. Go forth onto the holy ground, onto the ruins of the abbey and seek the site of Mary's grave. It is time to remember our past together." Yeshua explained that I had incarnated with a great responsibility to unify the first 144,000 into "the secret of the lion—I came as the lamb, I return as the lion, henceforth, within your message they will discover why they have come. Within the light of the father, in thy name they will find solace and their heartful relief in that they are fulfilling their promise to God. Go in peace my brother."

I understood. I felt the true feeling of freedom after my soulmerging experience. I was so excited and overwhelmed yet thrilled by the revelation that Yeshua just shared with me. I returned the blue sapphire chalice to the innkeeper. I briefly shared the appearance of Yeshua confirming that indeed the same cup that Joseph of Arimathea buried so long ago. I decided to keep the rest of the information to myself. Exhausted from traveling, I decided to take a short walk and then turn in for the night. I walked up Tor Hill. It was legend that the Celtic shamans held a mystery school at the base of the hill. Also, it was said a huge spiraling labyrinth and energy vortex is present under Tor Hill. I arrived at the top and instantly felt the inter-dimensional doorway open. At the center of my solar plexus I felt powerful earth energies rise up through my body and simultaneously I felt light descend from the higher dimensions above me. The light flowed down through my crown meeting the powerful earth energies in my solar plexus. "As above, so below." No wonder in ancient days before Christ this was a center for Celtic, pagan religion. It is difficult for a young initiate on the path of healing to open the base chakra, this is where fear resides. But here at The Tor, the energy of this holy ground makes it easier to transmute fear, allowing divine light to enter. I walked back to the Chalice Well Inn recalling my lifelong intrigue with the Arthurian legends, Knights of the Round Table and the quest for the Holy Grail.

Is it possible Yeshua had just revealed the truth of the Holy Grail and the true meaning of the Cross? After all these years, I thought the Cross meant the eternal suffering of man's inhumanity to man but there was a deeper meaning. When we allow ourselves to open and our trust and faith in ourselves is great enough we can become the chalice. WE ARE THE CUP! But the secret has been kept from us. By purifying the vessel (the wounds of the past), we can begin to literally access and merge with the light of the soul, and our deep connection to God.

As I thought of this revelation, love filled every part of my being. I could feel this love came directly from Yeshua, confirming the truth of his message. I was humbled and in a profound state of awe! When I awoke the next morning, I could not wait to enter the ancient ruins of Glastonbury. I entered the ruins and hurried to find the burial site of Mary. I sat down as Yeshua instructed. It was early morning and very few tourists were at the site and so my meditation was uninterrupted. Mother Mary appeared alongside of Yeshua, she said, "We drew you to this sacred site for a very important reason— to help you retrieve part of your soul memory, a time when we were a family together. I would like to make a point of clarification."

Tears welled up in my eyes as I sat in her energetic embrace. She continued, "This was the burial site of Miriam, one of my Essene sisters." She went on to explain that she had lived out her days in the south of France, near the modern day Saint-Maximin-La Sainte Baume, at which time she was accompanied by Mary Magdalene. It was at this moment I fell very deep into my meditation and a great memory began to unfold. I began to recall a prior life where Yeshua and I were in our late teens. We were accompanied by our mother Mary, and Joseph of Arimathea and others to this very site. There were seven of us: Mother Mary, Mary Magdalene, Yeshua, James, Joseph of Arimathea, Salome and Ruth. Who was I? I wondered. Mother Mary and Yeshua both resounded, "James Ben Joseph." She said, "There, it is done. Blessed be you my son. Peace be with you my brother." I asked, "Could this be true? What do I do with this revelation?" Yeshua answered, "Write it down. It is part of your message." Then they both faded away. When the vision was over I went back to my room and fell asleep. When I awoke, I began to write the Great Vision as it came to me.

THE GREAT VISION

YESHUA, HIS BROTHER JAMES, THEIR MOTHER MARY, MARY MAGDELENE, SALOME, RUTH AND JOSEPH OF ARIMETHEA WERE VISITED BY ARCHANGEL GABRIEL. IT WASN'T THE FIRST TIME GABRIEL HAD COME WITH INSTRUCTIONS INVOLVING THEIR PART IN THE DIVINE

PLAN; HOWEVER, THIS TIME THERE WAS SOMETHING DIFFERENT, FILLING THEM WITH THE GRAVITY OF KNOWING THEIR LIVES WERE ABOUT TO CHANGE FOREVER.

GABRIEL INSTRUCTED THEM TO CROSS THE GREAT SEA AND HEAD TOWARD THE GREEN ISLES. SPECIFICALLY, THEY WERE TO GO TO THE ISLE OF AVALON (TODAY'S GLASTONBURY) UNTIL THEY CAME UPON A GOLDEN WHITE RAY EMANATING FROM THE HEAVENS AND ENTERING EARTH ON HOLY GROUND. UPON THE ISLE OF AVALON BENEATH THE RAY OF LIGHT, THEY WOULD COME TO A CIRCLE. THEY WERE TO WAIT THERE FOR A GRAND VISION OF THEIR FUTURE LIFE—THEN AND IN **2012 AND BEYOND**. THIS VISION WOULD APPEAR TO THEM OVER A PERIOD OF SEVEN DAYS.

TRAVEL THEY DID ACROSSS THE GREAT SEA WITH JOSEPH OF ARIMETHEA TO THE SHORES OF ENGLAND. WHILE MANY MILES OUT TO SEA, THEY WERE ALL WITNESS TO THE GOLDEN RAY, THE RADIANCE OF WHICH COULD BE FELT IN THE HEARTS OF EACH. IT STRANGELY MAGNETIZED IN THEM A HEARTFELT RESONANCE THAT CALLED TO THEM, PULLING THEM TOWARD IT. AS THEY ARRIVED, THEY CAME INTO A

CIRCLE WITHIN THE RAY AND WAITED AS ARCHANGEL GABRIEL HAD INSTRUCTED.

PREPARING FOR SOULMERGING

SOON GABRIEL APPEARED WITHIN THE BRILLIANT PRESENCE OF MULTICOLORED OPALESCENT DIVINE LIGHT TO BEGIN PREPARING THEIR PHYSICAL BODIES FOR SOULMERGING AND THE GREAT VISION. THEY WOULD RECEIVE A VISION OF THE FUTURE BY DIVINE DECREE, DIRECTLY FROM GOD—THE LIGHT OF THE FATHER, THE LIGHT OF LIGHTS, THE LOVE THAT LOVES AND THE HOLY OF HOLIES. THROUGH GABRIEL'S PRESENCE, LIGHT BEGAN RIVETING THROUGH THEIR BODIES TO THE MAXIMUM THRESHOLD OF EACH INDIVIDUAL'S CAPACITY, SATURATING THEM WITH HIGH-VIBRATORY CASCADING WAVES OF LIGHT, LOVE AND PURE CONSCIOUSNESS.

GABRIEL SAID IT WAS SOON TIME TO SOULMERGE. THIS WOULD AMPLIFY THE LIGHT ALREADY WITHIN, BATHE THEM IN LOVE AND PURIFY THEIR BEINGS. LIGHT EMERGED FROM THEIR SEVEN INNER CENTERS, DANCING THROUGH THE AIR AND THE SURROUNDING SPACE. THEY BEHELD SPLENDID RAYS OF GOLDEN LIGHT AND RAREFIED HUES OF WHITE AND PINKISH BLUE. AS

CELESTIAL VEILS WERE OPENING IN MID-AIR, DIMENSIONAL DOORWAYS BEAMED THROUGH THE PRESENCE OF MANY LORDS OF LIGHT, SAINTS AND ASCENDED MASTERS, GUARDIANS OF THE RAYS OF TRANSFORMATION.

DURING THIS PREPARATION, GABRIEL EXPLAINED THE TWELVE CREATIONAL RAYS OF LIGHT. THEY ARE WHITE, PINK, GREEN, RED, YELLOW, MAGENTA, BLUE AND BLUE-WHITE, THE REMAINING ARE DIFFUSED SUBTLER VARIATIONS OF BLUE, WHITE-GOLD AND PINKISH-ORANGE. FINALLY, THE LAST RAY IS THE BLUE-BLACK RAY OF PURE CONSCIOUSNESS, WHICH IS LIKE THE MIDNIGHT BLUE OF A STARRY NIGHT. IN TOTAL, THEY MAKE UP YOUR SUBTLE LIGHT BODY WHICH CREATES THE LIGHT TEMPLATE OF YOUR PHYSICAL BODY. DIVINE RAYS ALSO DESCEND INTO MANY PLACES OVER THE EARTH IN EVERY COUNTRY AND ARE OFTEN LOCATED NEAR TEMPLE RUINS, ANCIENT MYSTERY SCHOOLS AND PLACES OF ONGOING WORSHIP. YOU MAY DISCOVER THEM IF YOU HAVE EYES TO SEE, BUT THE HEART ALWAYS FEELS THEIR PRESENCE.

SUDDENLY, WITH A WAVE-LIKE GESTURE FROM GABRIEL, THE KNOWLEDGE HELD WITHIN THE RAYS ENTERED THE VISITORS' CROWN CHAKRAS. HE

173

PROPHESIED THAT THOSE PRESENT WOULD LATER ENCOUNTER MANY GUIDED JOURNEYS THROUGHOUT THE WORLD. THEY WOULD COMMUNE WITH, MERGE WITH AND RECEIVE KNOWLEDGE AND INITIATIONS THROUGH STREAMS OF LIGHT, FURTHERING THEIR CHRISTING (THE UNION OF LOVE AND LIGHT WITHIN THE PHYSICAL). EACH RAY OF LIGHT IS UNIQUE AND CONTAINS THE WISDOM OF THE STARS. THE HEART FEELS THE RAYS AS AN INVITATION TO PURIFY A PART OF ONE'S EXISTENCE, ALWAYS RESULTING IN THE DIRECT EXPERIENCE OF ILLUMINATION.

SECOND DAY OF LIGHT-INFUSIONS

AFTER HOURS OF LIGHT STREAMING IN THE PRESENCE OF GABRIEL AND THE FATHER, THE LIGHT OF LIGHTS, THEY WERE ASKED TO REST AND RETURN THE FOLLOWING MORNING. UPON RISING, THEY WERE STUNNED TO FIND THEIR BODIES PHYSICALLY AGLOW. EACH COULD ACTUALLY SEE THE OTHERS' LUMINOSITY, AND EACH WAS NEAR EXHAUSTION, YET STRANGELY EXHILARATED. THEY REASSEMBLED INTO A CIRCLE AND WAITED.

THE EARTH BEGAN TO TREMBLE FROM IMMENSE MAGNETIC WAVES OF PULSING ENERGY,

RHYTHMICALLY RADIATING THROUGH THEIR FEET AND UP ALL THE WAY OUT THEIR CROWNS. YESHUA AND JAMES BOTH HAD TROUBLE GROUNDING AT FIRST, BUT MARY AND MARY MAGDELENE, ALONG WITH SALOME, HELD THE BROTHERS' FEET UNTIL THEY WERE ATTUNED TO THE NEW EXPANDED STATE AND MORE SETTLED INTO THEIR BODIES. THE LIGHT FROM THE PREVIOUS DAY WAS SO INTENSE AND PHYSICALLY EXPANSIVE THAT THEY ALL FELT QUITE PRESENT, YET HOLOGRAPHICALLY AT-ONE WITH "ALL THERE IS." JOSEPH, MUCH LIKE THE SALT OF THE EARTH, HELD THE ENTIRE CIRCLE IN PERFECT ALIGNMENT BY HIS GROUNDED, FATHER-LIKE PRESENCE.

COMING TO A MOMENTARY REST, EACH TRAVELER FELT PHYSICALLY REVITALIZED AND READY FOR WHAT WAS NEXT. AGAIN THEIR HEARTS BEGAN TO VIBRATE WITH RADIATING LIGHT UNTIL EACH INDIVIDUAL LIGHT PRESENCE CAME INTO UNION WITH THE OTHERS. THEY BECAME ONE LARGE CIRCLE OF TORUS-SHAPED LIGHT, FORMING A BRILLIANT GEOMETRIC DONUT THAT UNFOLDED IN A CONTINUUM ONTO ITSELF. THE CIRCLE OF SEVEN BECAME ONE BODY OF LIGHT IN "AT-ONEMENT."

TO THEIR SURPRISE, THROUGH TRANSLUSCENT VEILS THEY BEGAN TO SEE OCEANS OF LIGHT BEINGS SURROUNDING THEM IN SUPPORT. SUDDENLY, THEY BEHELD A TREMENDOUS CORRIDOR OF LIGHT, FILLED WITH THE ENERGY OF LOVE. THEY STOOD MOTIONLESS FROM AN ALL PREVADING TELEPATHIC INFUSION THAT BECAME AN INNER VISION WHICH REVEALED FUTURE EVENTS OF THE SECOND COMING—EMANATING, FLOWING AND PULSING CONTINUOUSLY. VIRTUAL LIVING LIGHT FROM COUNTLESS DIMENSIONS UNVEILED THEIR FUTURE AND THE EVOLUTION OF COLLECTIVE HUMANITY IN THE MODERN DAY.

THEIR HEARTS WERE POUNDING BECAUSE OF SO MUCH LOVE FROM GABRIEL AND THE ATTENDING ARCHANGELS—RAPHAEL, MICHAEL, METATRON, ARIEL AND SANDALPHON. QUICKLY BRUSHING TEARS FROM THEIR EYES SO AS NOT TO MISS ANY DETAILS, THE SEVEN BLESSED ONES GATHERED CLOSER. THEY HAD BARELY COMPOSED THEMSELVES WHEN AN IMMENSE LIGHT APPEARED. IT COMPLETELY CIRCLED THE GOLDEN-WHITE RAY WITH MAGNIFICENCE. SATURATED WITH THE DEEPEST PEACE IMMAGINABLE, THEY ENTERED A TIMELESS EXPANSE. THEY FELT NO SEPARATION IN THIS VAST UNIFYING REALITY, WHICH

SUSPENDED GRAVITY WITHIN THE CLEAR, FLUIDIC CANVAS OF LIGHT.

WITHOUT WARNING, THEY WITNESSED THE FIRST SCENES OF FUTURE EVENTS BURSTING FORTH FROM THE SPLENDOR. THE GROUP LOOKED AHEAD TO THE SECOND MILLENNIUM (2012) AND A WORLDWIDE SUBATOMIC INFUSION OF LIGHT. THIS INFLUX HELD A NEW CONSCIOUSNES, DEFINED BY MULTIPLE PULSE-WAVING RINGS THAT CIRCUMNAVIGATED THE EARTH AND SPIRALED OUT TO THE STARS. THE PURE BLAZE WAS EMANATING FROM 144 LIGHT-INCEPTED BEINGS—THEIR FELLOW ESSENES—WHO WOULD IN 2012 BECOME THE FIRST 144,000 TO HOLD THE HIGHER VIBRATIONAL OCTAVE AS A RESULT OF SOULMERGING.

THE ESSENES BEGAN TO REALIZE THE IMPORTANCE OF THE VISION. IN THE FUTURE (TODAY'S PRESENT), NO MATTER WHERE ON EARTH, THEY WOULD LINK TO ALL INITIATES AND THUS REACH A NEW ZENITH OF EFFULGENCE. THEY WERE GENESIS TO A HOST OF STAR-SEEDED BEINGS, SPARKING THE MOMENTUM OF LIGHT THAT WOULD TRIGGER A LEAP IN HUMAN EVOLUTION. THIS CONSCIOUS SPIRITUAL AWAKENING WOULD BE KNOWN AS THE "RETURN OF THE LION" OR "THE SECOND COMING."

AMID OVERWHELM AND AWE, THE SEVEN VISITORS TO GLASTONBURY CONTINUOUSLY ABSORBED THE ONENESS OF THE LIGHT, FASHIONED BY THE TUBE-LIKE TORUS SURROUNDING THEM IN CONTINUUM. FOR THE DIVINE TRUTH TO MANIFEST, IT HAD TO BE IMPRINTED ONTO THEIR DNA. THEY NEEDED TO REMEMBER IT, BECOME IT, AND IGNITE THE FIRST LIGHT INITIATIONS AND SOULMERGINGS WITHIN THE ORIGINAL ESSENES. THE BLESSED ONES WITH YESHUA AND JAMES WERE RECEIVING PROFOUND TELEPATHIC COMMUNICATION ON MANY LEVELS. THEY WOULD SOON SERVE AS AN INNER GROUP WITHIN THE LARGER CIRCLE OF 144 LIGHT-INCEPTED ESSENES, WHO WOULD THEN ALL BE ABLE TO ACCESS THE EVER-STREAMING GOLDEN HUES, THE LIGHT OF THE SOUL.

THE MAGNITUDE OF THE VISION

THE LIGHT-INFUSING PREPARATION FOR SOULMERGING, GUIDED BY ARCHANGEL GABRIEL, HAD STIMULATED THE HEART OF THE TRAVELERS. IT ALSO TAUGHT THEM BY DIRECT EXPERIENCE HOW TO MAINTAIN THEIR FOCUS AND RE-LIVE THIS MOMENT AT WILL. BY DOING SO, THEY WOULD ALWAYS HAVE ACCESS TO THE VERY SAME DIVINE CORRIDOR THAT

WAS BEFORE THEM. THEY COULD EXPAND THEIR AURAS TO A PLACE BEYOND THE THIRD DIMENTION, YET BY DEEP CONCENTRATION THEY COULD ALSO BRING ALONG THEIR PHYSICAL BODIES. ENTERING INTO THE LIGHT OF HEAVEN, THEY MANIFEST HEAVEN ON EARTH, OR "THY KINGDOM COME, ON EARTH AS IT IS IN HEAVEN."

NOW THEY BECAME AWARE OF EVEN DEEPER LEVELS OF MEANING WITHIN THEIR FEELING BODIES. THEY ACCEPTED A NEW SENSE OF AWARENESS IN THAT LIVING LIGHT, AWAKENING TO THE INFINITE NATURE OF THEIR SOUL DESIGN AND THE TRUTH OF THEIR MISSION. BY THE SECOND MILLENNIUM, THERE WOULD BE THREE TIMES 144,000 OR 432,000 HUMANS WITH THE POTENTIAL TO IGNITE THE REST OF HUMANITY. BEING IN THE FIRST WAVE WOULD NOT BE EASY, HOWEVER, FOR THEY WOULD NEED TO OVERCOME GREAT INNER CHALLENGES!

BREATHLESS AND GASPING, YESHUA AND JAMES REELED. THE SIGNIFICANCE OF THEIR PART IN THE DIVINE PLAN PENETRATED THROUGH TO THEIR AWARENESS WHILE TEARS SWELLED. THEY EMBRACED EACH OTHER, FOR IT WAS REVEALED THAT JAMES WAS TO EMBODY THE ABSOLUTE PURITY OF ALL SEVEN RAYS

OF LIGHT. HE WOULD BE A PILLAR TO YESHUA, WHO WAS TO EMBODY ABSOLUTE, UNCONDITIONAL LOVE. MOTHER MARY WOULD HOLD THE ENERGY OF PURITY (INNOCENCE), MARY MAGDELENA WOULD HOLD UNCONDITIONAL LOVE AS THE DIVINE FEMININE; RUTH, ABSOLUTE FAITH; SALOME, ENDURING TRUST; AND JOSEPH, THE DIVINE MALE. TOGETHER THEY WOULD EMBODY THE "ARC OF THE COVENANT." IN UNION, THESE SEVEN WOULD BRIDGE THE HIGHEST VIRTUES THROUGHOUT THEIR EARTHLY MISSION AND MERGE PHYSICALLY WITH THE HOLY OF HOLIES, PURE DIVINE CONSCIOUSNESS.

EACH OF THE CHOSEN WITHIN THE CIRCLE WAS ASKED TO RADIATE THE VIRTUE OF A CERTAIN RAY AND WOULD, IN ONE LIFETIME, TRANSMUTE THE ABSOLUTE POLARITY OF THAT ESSENCE—ITS DISTORTION, OR ANTI-LIGHT. EVEN THOUGH SOME OF THEM WERE VERY YOUNG, THEY WOULD RECEIVE MULTIPLE INITIATIONS OR PASSAGES INTO LIGHT, PURIFYING THEIR HUMAN NATURE. THEY WOULD COME TOGETHER WITH OTHERS TO DISPEL THE COLLECTIVE NATURE OF OPPOSITES, THE SEVEN CORE WOUNDS AND MANY EGOIC STATES OR DISTORTIONS THAT ENCUMBER EARTHLY EXISTENCE. THEY LEARNED TO BE AS ONE, TO GO BEYOND VARIOUS HUMAN HISTORIES THAT CAN DIVIDE THE COLLECTIVE.

BEGINNING WITH THEMSELVES, THEY TRANSFORMED THE PAST, PRESENT AND FUTURE OF MAN'S INHUMANITY TO MAN AS WELL AS THE SEPARATION CAUSED BY THE MALE-FEMALE RELATIONSHIP, FROM WITHIN AND WITHOUT. AND THEN THEY HELPED OTHERS TO DO THE SAME, CREATING A MOMENTUM OF LIGHT THAT IS EXPLODING EXPONENTIALLY IN THIS NEW MILLENNIUM.

The entire Great Vision is referred to as "The Three Great Waves of Light." According to the vision, the Light causes a genesis in time, called the "Great Shift," an awakening of humanity and the ushering in The Kingdom of God. The Great Shift is known as "The End of Days and the End of Time." At a specific moment, all life will evolve in a spiritual leap of consciousness to a more expanded, higher-vibrational human existence.

CHAPTER 14

THE PROMISE TO GOD

Are You One of the 144,000?

A profound message from the soul memory of James Ben Joseph regarding the ancient ones who are alive today and here to assist in the Awakening of Humanity...

The Second Coming . . . The Momentum of Light

The descendants of the Essenes have returned to fulfill their promise to God, the Light of the Father. Two millennia later, the descendants of the first 144 Essenes have multiplied into a thousand times three, creating three waves of 144,000 descendants who were destined to enter the Soulmerging experience in the modern day. They are alive now and creating a total of 432,000 who are Soulmerging into their light bodies. Together, these three waves of light will lead to a tipping point within collective consciousness, making it easier for all of humanity to Soulmerge and evolve into the New Human. **The second coming is not a person, but a group!** As they remember how to access divine light, these awakening souls are creating an unstoppable Momentum of Light.

What the Bible refers to as "The End of Days and the End of Time" also known as "The Great Shift of the Ages" is in process now! This momentum will reach its peak beginning in 2012, the end of the Mayan calendar, and over three-to-five years thereafter. Concurrently, there is an unprecedented solar and celestial alignment that is about to birth a new sun in the fourth dimension. Stellar events are precipitating an evolutionary step for humanity and, indeed, all life on many levels. On earth, lower-vibratory human energy—physical, emotional and mental bodies—is transmuting to an accelerated rate —due to the illumination that is occurring within the spiritual body—causing the expansion of the human auric energy fields. We are becoming the New Humans; beings who are no longer fear-based, but rather heart-centered.

Anna, mother of Mary, grandmother of Yeshua and James, was an Immortal who knew the sacred arts and the secrets of being at-one with divine light. During two generations, she was an instrument to "light incept" (what the Bible refers to as "immaculate conception") 72 males and 72 females, totaling 144. These "Children of Light" included Mary, Yeshua and James. The secrets of divine light were held in sacred scrolls and the Tables of Osiris in Egypt, where initiates early in history practiced the hidden rites. Anna brought the teachings from Alexandria to the Essenes in Jerusalem. The most sacred of these was how to access inner and outer light directly. With much preparation, the Children of Light began raising their energy by a series of initiations, such as Soulmerging. Once many of them had moved to fourth- and fifth-level vibrational mastery, the individuals gradually began to merge as a group! Thus, the first 144 were blessed by the presence of group radiance, love energy that was electric, to say the least. They lived within a community where each person radiated his or her unique golden essence to form one heart. From that time forward, they carried a profound urge throughout earthly life to initiate the union of love and light within.

Archangel Gabriel revealed the Divine Plan to Anna and the Essenes by demonstrating how to reach divine union as a group, thereby creating the Momentum of Light. The higher vibratory rate of the uplifted initiates was meant to radiate exponentially throughout collective humanity, resulting in more Love consciousness! However, the children of light did not complete their divine purpose in one lifetime. Union was achieved by only a core group, including Yeshua, who was the closest to merging his physical body with divine, unconditional Love. He entered into the cosmic Christ consciousness, assisted by members of the core circle, including Mary Magdalene, who served to hold him energetically.

Yeshua's words, "I came as the Lamb; I return as the Lion," refer to the centuries of increasing light on Earth. Divine light enthralled a small group called the Children of Light (Lamb) but is returning as the unstoppable energy of their many descendents (Lion). Once 144,000 enter the Soulmerging experience, many others will spontaneously Soulmerge as memories bubble to the surface of their awareness. The first ones to awaken are reporting unusual extrasensory, empathic and mystical experiences. In the process of transmuting and healing, many emotional and physical traumas are being lifted along the way.

Everything is made of creational energy—love, light and pure consciousness! We are actually co-creating with this energy, reflecting outward with our every thought, emotion, act and deed! During early life, however, most humans are subjected to emotional wounding, such as fear, judgment, manipulation and critical treatment, which is held energetically in the subconscious and unconscious as memory. The accumulation of layers of internalized painful memories (or anti-light) darkens and contracts a person's auric energy field. Our naturally high vibration is lowered, leaving us with heavy burdens of suffering. Memories of love, happiness and joy remain luminous within our energy field.

Anywhere you see the word *antichrist* in the Bible, you can substitute its true meaning: Anti-light! Christ consciousness is a state of being and not limited to a particular person. The Christed state manifests from intentional awareness in union with the Love and Light of the Father. This Holy Communion or holy alignment can be felt and entered at will after you transmute the majority of emotional burdens that hide within. Entering the inner golden essence, or Heaven on Earth, is made possible through the secret teachings, which impart the miracle of Soulmerging. Rediscovery of this divine birthright was not welcomed in every quarter, however. Under siege and distorted deliberately, the teachings went underground for many centuries, waiting to be remembered at the ideal time.

The descendants of the 144 are healing the seven core wounds of humanity. This process can be difficult and life disrupting, causing the first who Soulmerge to undergo continuous transformation. They must stretch to deeper and deeper levels of trust and faith while unraveling old identities and patterns. Because

185

they are in the first wave, these individuals often feel as if the sequences of change will take forever. However, they *will* reach the Soulmerge and further initiations of light, especially by being around others who have already integrated this experience!

Inner soul purging of the past can mimic both common and extraordinary physical, mental and emotional experiences. For example, many recall seeing angelic light beings or the energy of light. Others feel magnetically drawn to travel, a strong affinity to cultures of the past and meeting many people along the way. Meanwhile, each initiate is remembering the soul knowledge of accessing the divine! Even one's dream and sleep time is active with healing. Not a moment is wasted because all feel the urgent need to fulfill an extraordinary purpose. To implement the divine plan of Heaven on Earth, the sacred union with Self must be accomplished. Then one proceeds to union with all souls who have returned to renew the world through The Momentum of Light.

The descendants of the Essenes and all other initiates, and all of humanity are beginning to enter the long-awaited Divine Encounter. Soulmerging is an extraordinary moment of transformation, not just a spiritual metaphor. It entails seeing and feeling the golden light of the soul with physical eyes while feeling profound waves of Love in a succession of heart openings. It is the overwhelming experience of being in the physical presence of God! The golden light of the soul streams into the crown and down to the chakra beneath the feet. This splendid event can last for hours, causing rapture in the wake of accelerated healing light, love and pure consciousness! The physical body is imbued with the light of the soul, or Three Faces of God, known as the Holy Trinity: Divine Light, Divine Love and Pure Consciousness. Your present life and many former lifetimes flash before your eyes as multiple levels of burdens rapidly transmute within the soul's causal body. According to Archangel Gabriel, as of November 2011, 76,487 humans have entered the Soulmerge.

Those who awakened at the time of Christ kept the Great Vision a secret. They embodied on earth with light encoded in their DNA to protect the sacred arts and keep their divine purpose from members of religious orders who would distort the truth. Now they have reached the assured acceleration of their vehicles of light. In the future, we will live in high-vibrational radiance, naturally accessing our fourth- and fifth-dimensional selves. At-one with essence, we can naturally enter the source of inner intuition, automatic knowingness, love and light, where love instead of fear leads the way. Original innocence will flow in effortless forethought that loves without judgment or placing value upon the objects of our loving.

The Language of Energy and Light

Those who were light incepted into third-dimensional earth did not automatically enter their divinity, however. They still needed the Soulmerge and ongoing initiations of light to integrate new levels of vibrational awareness into daily life. This was made possible by maintaining the holy alignment within—individually and as a group with unified intention.

The Essenes lived from the center of their being, their essence. They were able to focus on their soul light stream, a most natural golden radiance that penetrates deep into the chakras, sourcing from the multidimensional God Self (fourth- through sixth-dimensional interactive consciousness). The ability to enter at-onement is necessary to navigate third-dimensional reality with ease. We require intuitive mental discernment and familiarity with the energy signatures of the feeling body. This Way of the Heart allows us to co-create with innocence and imagination.

Transmuting deep core wounds profoundly and permanently will change your life as you know it. A new lightness of being deepens your ability to accept, allow, love and embrace your inner and outer reality. Previous emotional reactions that seemed out of your control simply melt away as you repair burdens triggered by the following thought forms:

1. Fear/Death
2. Conditional Love
3. Rejection/Separation
4. Disempowerment/Power
5. Distrust/Intimacy/Authenticity
6. Trust/Distrust
7. Judgment/Acceptance

We have the natural ability to communicate, commune or merge with the spiritual essence of the four temples of earth, namely, mineral, water, air and fire-light. All earth elemental essences have energy and light that can be directly experienced. Where the earth has not been adulterated, you will find powerful energies that surround your awareness with wisdom and healing. These are not occasional mystical experiences but every day, fourth-dimensional interactive states that nurture your physical body. Humanity is cut off from these natural elemental forces when mental energy states of fear, anger, hatred or judgment are present. This is the way most people live today.

You will become more interactive with yourself by listening deliberately, that is, by residing in the heart-mind of your feeling body. In the time of Christ this was known as "The Living Way;" living from essence, you feel your way through life. Practically, this means to listen, to feel and then you will know. In this way, you open yourself to the rich experience of communing with nature. The miracle of the physical body awaits you as it consistently transmits profound elemental wisdom. It naturally lets you know what it needs at all times, including what to stay away from. It will signal when you need love or nurturing and what food and drink are necessary. Many times this can impress a mental image that can be felt and seen as, "I just know."

Communication with earth is vital to understanding that we are the same energy and light essence that makes up earth, water, trees and so on. As you connect to the elemental energy in your body, you can easily communicate with the cells. The physical body is affected by three overlapping bodies of energy—our mental, emotional and spiritual or light bodies. If we do not thoroughly know the other energetic bodies and how they affect us, our physical body becomes highly susceptible to dis-ease and suffering. However, you can heal any state of disease through self-loving communion.

The Essenes knew that the physical body is the endpoint of light. They knew about the twelve overlapping spheres of light, each one vibrating at a different level. At the center of each sphere is a chakra. The energy goes into vibrational resonance with the rays of creation in the third dimension, then into the etheric templates of life, and finally, into our physical body. This knowledge made it possible for them to be interactive with self energetically. By learning all the energy signatures of each subtle body and focusing on their central alignment, the Essenes were able to self-illuminate. This is what Socrates meant when he said, "Know Thyself!" and what Yeshua meant by, "When you know yourselves, then you will be known, and you will understand that you are children of the Living Father!"

To enter holy alignment, they brought their hands together, creating two overlapping triangles of golden energy. It is little known even today that one can achieve pure consciousness by clasping the hands over the heart in a prayerful way. When one is focused this way, the energy of Divine Mind and the One Heart is superimposed over the physical body, forming the Star of David or two golden triangles within the auric energy field. While in holy alignment and with eyes upturned, the pineal gland secrets a hormone that increases one's vibratory energy into the fourth and fifth dimensions.

With prayerful intention "for the highest good of all," the Essenes would utilize the art of invocation. This was a focus upon, the calling forth of the divine father and mother in at-onement in order to merge with the unified field and then into the Christ grid and the "All There Is." Using the body temple of prayerful intention and focus, one begins to usher the soul into the divine template of the unified field, thereby accessing the union of creational light rays and pure consciousness. This union is what we call God: the energy of what is and what will be, a magnificent rapture of intense golden light satiated with love and all knowing. What surrounds us is the universal mind of God, creationally and magnetically potentializing a genesis that is just waiting to manifest our thoughts, feelings, intentions and inner beliefs, consciously and unconsciously. The early initiates knew they were co-creating with the God Force because they had discovered this all-intelligent power was also within them, flowing unendingly. They knew the unseen qualities of universal creation were real and accessible by being reverently interactive, accessing the higher-vibrational fields to which our human auric energy is already connected. Becoming interactive with creation is the deeper meaning of faith, as in **"faith applied."**

The Essenes found Peace Beyond Understanding, which showed in faces that beamed humble but passionate joy. In almost every instant, they were in the moment, not in the past or the future. As a result, their conscious awareness, their essence, was able to reside in higher sense perception. Their relationship to others was clear also because they honored the feeling body, sometimes called abiding in Living Truth. When one exists in this fourth-dimensional state, divine mind is able to flow effortlessly. Intuition and automatic knowing are available without ever thinking and without judgment, expectation or assigning value. This purer state of being is our most natural state, in sync with "All There Is."

The Essenes had direct access to soul knowledge, soul guidance, soul creativity and a level of causeless joy that in modern times is thought not to be possible. By letting their soul uniqueness unfold in the endless wonderment of interactive allowance, they also enjoyed the ability to merge with the light of their extended family; therefore, the light of each soul joined as One—in everyday life and in community! This was the beginning of the new family of man, the New Earth. Living in this high energy, they were filled with light, the amplified essence of themselves within the greater community. As co-creators of reality, they yearned to be responsible and accountable for their actions, knowing that every spoken word, inner thought and heartfelt belief would soon be on its way to manifestation.

Ridding the egoic mind of unnecessary thoughts and, even more important, spoken words, was essential. The Essenes reverently offered prayerful forethought for the "highest good of all," known and unknown, choosing to see beauty first with positive, open acceptance in every aspect of life. This was freedom lived. When uncomfortable emotions came, they accepted them as signals from the inner self that they were out of alignment. In contrast, positive emotions of hope, happiness, wonderment, passion and creativity would pour out when they were flowing in the fulfillment of the heart.

Archangel Gabriel says, "All is given according to your belief!" Where then, do beliefs come from? First ask, are they *your* beliefs or someone else's? What about unconscious beliefs? Beliefs are something you have placed value upon and become identified with. Unconscious beliefs are values and identities held in deep memory. Although we have forgotten about them, they nevertheless are driving unconscious behavior, reactions and physical dis-ease. Why do we egoically identify ourselves with expectations and demands from the past that cause us to feel less than or superior to others? Why not just be? Beliefs that cause suffering are from core wounds. They are what drive the egoic mind and override the wisdom of our divine mind. The Essenes knew the difference.

When a soul chooses to birth into human form, "light-incepted" or not, it must pass through the heaviness of the astral layer surrounding earth. This psychic airway holds the magnetic thought forms of collective humanity. Laden with the core wounds of existence in the body, these mind projections pull heavily on the virtuous nature of incarnating souls, dimming their divine light or essence. To surmount this anti-light requires great vigilance and discernment.

In collective humanity there is a dream common to all—a dream of being free in a better tomorrow, hope of joy, love, happiness and existing with passion for life in the energy of aliveness. We long to be one with the beauty within all life, inside and out. We seek liberation in a body that is an instrument, a chalice or cup that overfloweth. We never lose the knowing that some day we will get there: Heaven on Earth. Where does this common dream come from? It already exists within every soul in the fourth-dimension, a higher energetic state of being. However, you must align with the energy of the inner soul to get there. It is not easy, yet it is simple. You have to want it, intend it and choose it.

The divine potential of the Essenes was to ascend as a group while still in their physical bodies; they hoped to pass through the many mystical thresholds of enlightenment simultaneously into full soul-level existence, to realize the multidimensional self (third through the ninth levels) while still grounded in third-dimensional bodies. They had the potential to experience super consciousness or pure creational existence, at-onement and full communion with all. Based in love, they had dominion over the physical, entering the many thresholds of Christed being while living in the union of love and light. Even a group this small, 144 beings balanced between male and female, was enough to change the world as we knew it. While in holy alignment, they held absolute focus on inner group union while utilizing the art of invoking divine light from higher dimensions, and they partially succeeded. For years, they held this holy alignment, transmuting the energy of anti-light.

Ceremonially, they grouped into concentric circles, creating massive rings of light and exponentially affecting themselves and humanity worldwide. Many times, a core segment within the group would form at the center of the circles of light. These individuals were named and guided when the moment was right: Yeshua, James, Mary Magdalene, Mother Mary, Salome, Joseph of Arimathea and Ruth— all were directed by archangels. The unique radiance held by the circles would potentially create the Arc of the Covenant, a star-seed of infinite wavic light, pulsing to shift and transmute the anti-light of collective humanity. Our spiritual potential to evolve into higher-vibrational states was being activated. Accelerating and transmuting fear-based collective consciousness one light pulse at a time, this first group held the energy to prepare humanity for the leap into the God self. Thereafter, the spiritual light body lying dormant within every human on the planet would begin to vibrate at the forefront of his or her awareness.

The first Essenes did not attain group ascension, the highest potential within the divine plan. When this did not occur, each soul was filled with a sense of failed purpose because they had been facilitating each other for years, building divine momentum. There was only one who achieved ascension in the beginning: Yeshua Ben Joseph. He entered fully into and through the door of divine unconditional love with his fourth- and fifth-dimensional light body. This high-vibratory luminescence expanded his conscious awareness into multiple dimensions after the many heart openings of the Soulmerge. Yeshua was held purposefully in divine light according to the Essene custom of holding one another in holy alignment within the Circles of Light. While held continuously in this way, he was the first to potentialize his highest attribute according to his soul's uniqueness. James, Mary, Mary Magdalene, Salome, Ruth and Joseph were not far behind in actualizing their own ascension. But the larger group did not complete the mission as a whole.

James Ben Joseph was the second to ascend. His unique attribute was fully-realized divine light, the union of the divine rays of life. Mother Mary held the pure state of innocence, embodying Divine Mother. Mary Magdalene held the pure state of feminine power and, as Yeshua's mate, loved and facilitated him through every heart opening. Salome realized her purity in power through grace. Joseph held the sustaining and protective love of the Divine Father. Ruth held the absolute peace of Divine Mind as her soul uniqueness. The radiant, luminescent energy of each one was to be fully realized individually and then brought together into union with each other. In other words, the purpose was for each to possess the exalted multiple soul attributes of unconditional love, divine light, innocence, grace, and a fully-balanced divine male and female— Divine Father and Divine Mother. They were then to facilitate the other Essenes into the pure multi-facets of the One Heart. This momentum moved them through profound states of fear, envy, jealousy, doubt, distrust and self-deception. To clear this energy, it became a daily vigilance of each person to assist and support the others. The vibrational energy that remained created an observable glow or halo.

The Essenes began performing miracles of healing because they knew how to be in at-onement. Local prophets, fervent Pharisees and the Sanhedrin received visions about the coming Kingdom of God. This threatened those in both religious and secular power. The light generated by the 200 or so Essenes was beginning to reach the collective psyche, as it was meant to. Moreover, the energy generating from such group alignment was enhancing the channeling of the prophets. Those who would rule over the people did not want the people to realize that the Light of God was within them. Great fear and jealousy produced secret plotting, with many agents seeking the so-called leaders of the Essenes. Agents covertly reached and threatened their family members with the promise to persecute, torture and crucify them if they did not cooperate. Their intent was to coerce the "leaders" to dismantle this perceived threat of revolt. The authorities let fear of what they did not understand blind them to the Living Truth that the Kingdom of Heaven is within.

The powerful, yet gentle urge to ascend and transmute their core wounds continued as if by a magnetic force of God, building in momentum. However, when pressure and threats from the outside world began to mount within the Essene community, the energy of fear crept into a few, then to many. The crush of threats from religious leaders and the fear of torture began to impinge increasingly on the Essenes, seeping into their auric fields. Soon, the potential for them to ascend as a group was lost, causing crushing heart-felt pain and profound sadness. They had come so close to fulfilling their Divine purpose. The dark energies of fear dominated even further and then in a final blow the Essenes as a group felt and heard a worldwide gasp coming from collective consciousness. The higher levels of every human on earth came so close to entering a spiritual leap of consciousness. The yearning of collective humanity to enter its spiritual body and the One Heart was thus postponed to the second millennium.

However, the anticipation of reaching full union in the One Heart had reached the subconscious mind of everyone on earth. By this time, Yeshua fully realized his Soulmerging to the extent that he could no longer hold back his ascension. It was decided and decreed by God and the archangels that he would merge into divine, unconditional love, transmuting many of the core wounds of humanity. He put into motion, for the future of man, a new path known as the path of Crucifixion and Resurrection. During the crucifixion, the immense love generated by Yeshua was so powerful that it shook the earth. There was a resounding call from within the hearts of the Essenes, and they vowed to return in the future to fulfill the Divine plan. Their time to fulfill the Promise is now!

So Be It.

So It Is.

May Peace And Love Reign Again For All.

Amen.

Coming in 2012...The Second Tablet of Testimony

In this second book, continue to journey with Dr. Stainetti on his twelve year holy pilgrimage led by the Archangels and Jesus. During his first Soulmerging experience Archangel Gabriel had said, "For the next twelve years you will be receiving countless streams of light. You are being prepared to receive a message for all of humanity. Prepare yourself to travel." He was all too familiar with what "prepare yourself to travel" meant and so he knew another great mystery was about to unfold. However, he was not prepared for what was about to happen next.

During his second Soulmerging experience, he was visited by Jesus (Yeshua). He stated it was time to be together again and that He would be guiding Dr. Stainetti on a journey to many ancient sites in Nepal, Tibet, India and Egypt. He further went on to explain that they would be retracing their footsteps taken together so long ago during their lifetime as Essenes. He stated the Soulmerging experience was just the beginning and the initiations of light would continue into many thresholds of enlightenment. His true life purpose was about to be revealed.

Throughout the message within this book, you will discover what it is to experience an initiation of light, which may already be occurring in your life today. You will further learn about the challenges you face and the reasons why. Your own journey to awaken will continue to unfold as more missing pieces about your Divine purpose are revealed.

About the Author

Dr. Stainetti is an author, master healer and spiritual teacher. In this first work, SOULMERGING™, The Path of Healing, Dr. Stainetti details the process for healing core wounds, spiritual transformation, and the heart awakening into enlightenment; an enlightenment that ultimately leads to the discovery and personal experience of the Light of the Soul within you. Soulmerging is the Divine birthright of every human being on earth.

For over 20 years, Dr. Stainetti has facilitated large-scale spiritual healing conferences throughout the United States as well as maintaining a private healing practice in Santa Barbara, California. Divinely led by Archangel Gabriel, he traveled to over 12 countries where he experienced profound awakenings in the temples and sacred sites of countries such as: Tibet, Egypt, Peru, England, France, Belgium, Italy, Mexico, Canada, Nepal and the Yucatan. He also attended many sacred and holy Native American ceremonies throughout North America. According to Archangel Gabriel, these encounters with the Divine were all preparing him to receive a great message for humanity—The Momentum of Light, The Divine Plan Unfolding.

It was during his Soulmerging experience that Dr. Stainetti entered the light of all souls, which we call "Heaven," and he has been able to access this Divine light and maintain this holy alignment ever since. He is clairvoyant, clairaudient, an empath with fully opened third-eye vision, and he is able to energetically hold the hearts of many in a state of at-onement. He received these Divine gifts after the discovery of the light of his soul. Whether you are standing before him, at a distance or over the phone in a long distance healing session, you will feel Divine energy coursing through you while he is identifying and revealing the core wounds of your specific human condition. His Divine purpose is dedicated to bringing the message of Soulmerging to all of humanity.

Made in the USA
Charleston, SC
31 December 2011